✓ S0-AXK-684

KURT JOHNSTON
MARK OESTREICHER

::MY FRIENDS

MS+FRND
MIDDLE SCHOOL SURVIVAL SERIES

ZONDERVAN®

ZONDERVAN.com/
AUTHORTRACKER
follow your favorite authors.

www.invertbooks.com

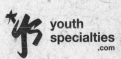
youth
specialties
.com

Youth Specialties products, 300 South Pierce Street, El Cajon, CA 92020,
are published by Zondervan, 5300 Patterson Avenue Southeast, Grand
Rapids, MI 49530.

Creative Team: Dave Urbanski, Laura Gross, Mark Novelli, Janie Wilkerson,
and Rich Cairnes
Cover design by Gearbox

Printed in the United States

09 10 11 12 • 10 9 8 7 6 5 4 3

DEDICATION

This book is dedicated to our two best friends from our own middle school years, two guys who (and this is amazing) are still two of our best friends, all these years later.

Marko's buddy was, and still is, John Mathers.

Kurt's buddy was, and still is, Mike Pace.

ACKNOWLEDGMENTS

Marko wants to thank his amazing family—Jeannie, Liesl, and Max. Thanks for being so loving and for your patience while I was writing. Thanks to my seventh grade guys' small group: Shane, Bryan, Lex, Matt, Zack, Aaron, and especially Brandon Matticks, whose last name I spelled wrong in the dedication of *My Family* because I'm still a dork.

Kurt wants to thank Rachel, Kayla, and Cole—you're not just my family; you really are my best friends. Thanks, also, to Matt Hall, who helped me when I was stuck (which seemed to happen quite often). You're a great friend, Matt!

CONTENTS

INTRODUCTION

See this really dorky picture right here? That's me, Marko, when I was in middle school. Nice shirt collar, huh? Can you tell I wasn't the most popular kid in school? Uh, yeah.

How about this groovy picture? That's me, Kurt, back during my middle school years. That haircut *rocked*, huh? Sure, whatever.

We wanted you to see those pictures—as embarrassing as they are—because we want you to know that we remember what it's like to be a middle school student. Partly, we remember because we've been working with middle schoolers in churches for a long time. We don't work with high school kids or with any other age group. That's because we're both convinced of a few things:

- First, middle schoolers are the coolest people in the world. Really! We'd rather hang out with a group of middle school students than any other age group.

- Next, God really cares (we mean, *REALLY CARES*) about middle school students—about you. And we believe God is stoked about the possibility of having a close relationship with you.

- Finally, the middle school years (from about 11 to 14 years old) are HUGELY important in building a FAITH that will last for your whole life.

This book is the third in a new series: The Middle School Survival Series. The first book is all about your faith (that's why it's called *My Faith*—duh!). The second book is about your family (it's called, not-so-surprisingly, *My Family*). The fourth book is also available now—it's called *My School*. And we have two more books planned for the series: *My Changes* and *My Future*. We hope you'll read them all!

Oh, one more thing: You don't have to read these 75 "chapters" in any particular order. It's not that kind of book. You *can* read them in order if you want to (if you're one of those people who likes order!); or you can just flip through and read whatever catches your attention.

We believe in you, and we'll be praying for you (really, we will) that while you read this, you'll grow in your understanding of God (just like the Bible says Jesus did when he was your age!), of how much God loves you, and of how God would do anything to let you know him!

Kurt and Marko

FRIENDSHIP BASICS

GOD'S DESIGN

Here's a wild thought: God created you to have friends. And friendship itself is something God thought up first.

See, God the Father, Jesus, and the Holy Spirit are all God, right? (We know this can be confusing, but stick with us.) We call that "the Trinity"—the three different "persons of God" who are still one.

Don't sweat it if that doesn't make sense to you. Just get this: Father, Son, and Holy Spirit all exist together in community—like an intense, committed friendship. So when God says in the Bible that we're made in his image (Genesis 1:26-27)—which just means we, in the deepest parts of who we are, share some similarities with the God who created us—then we must have that deep-friendship thing built into us.

You could say we're "wired" for friendship or we have the "programming" for friendship. But it's up to us to use it.

Think about this, too—God created everything that exists. Actually, first God thought of it, and *then* God created it. Laughter? Yup, God thought it up, and then created it. Palm trees? Yup, God thought them up, and then created them. Iguanas? Same thing. Families? Check. Friendship? I bet you can see where this is going.

So, when you read this book about friendship, and when you think about how you can be a better friend, and when you try to be a great friend or to make new friends, you're moving closer and closer to who God created you to be!

> "SCHOOL IS HARD. HOMEWORK IS HARDER.
> FINDING GREAT FRIENDS...EVEN HARDER.
>
> —TAYLOR, 8TH GRADE

SHIFTING FRIENDSHIPS

Now that you're moving into your middle school years, you may have noticed your friendships are changing. In fact, we've talked to hundreds of middle schoolers who struggle with this. Sometimes they feel guilty because they don't want to hang out with their childhood friends anymore. And sometimes they're pressured (by their parents, usually) to make different friends than the ones they already have.

Here's the scoop: You're changing. (Duh!) But really, you're changing BIG-time! In fact, except for the years between your birth and your third birthday, you're changing more *right now* than at any other time in your life. You're a change monster!

One thing that's changing the most is your brain (even though you sometimes feel like you've just lost it completely—or at least misplaced it for a little bit). Just like you're growing up physically—your body is changing and stuff like that—your brain is also growing up. One of the cool things about this brain change is that you're becoming unique. When we say *unique* we don't mean "weird" (although that may also be true!). We just mean you're becoming more *different* from other people—one of a kind.

Think of it this way: If you put a bunch of five-year-olds in a room with some toys, they'll pretty much all get along and play together (unless one kid is a total jerk-in-training who wants to make everyone miserable). But if you put a bunch of 13-

year-olds in a room with a CD player and a big stack of CDs, you're likely to hear, "I love this song!" at the same time you hear, "This song totally stinks!"

Little kids usually form friendships based on who lives near them or with whom they naturally spend a lot of time. But young teenagers form their friendships based on common interests (and this will remain true for the rest of your life). So lots of middle schoolers shift their reasons for having the friends they have from "because they live by me" to "because we like the same things."

This shift isn't easy. In fact, it's often messy. Feelings will probably get hurt. And misunderstandings are likely.

Here's what we want you to understand: The shifting-friendships thing is normal. It would be great for you to be loving and forgiving and all that stuff—both to new and old friends. But it's normal and okay to go through friendship changes during the middle school years.

"I HATE IT WHEN IN ELEMENTARY SCHOOL SOMEONE IS YOUR BEST FRIEND, BUT WHEN YOU GET TO MIDDLE SCHOOL THEY SUDDENLY THINK THEY'RE JUST TOO COOL FOR YOU."

—HALY, 7TH GRADE

CLIQUES

We wanted to talk about this topic at the beginning of the book because it's such a big deal in middle school. And it's WAY more of an issue than it was in grade school.

Some people call 'em *cliques* (pronounced "clicks"). You probably don't use that word; you probably call them "friendship groups." But there are different kinds of friendship groups, right? Some groups of friends are *open* and welcoming to new friends. Their attitude is, "Hey, if you want to hang with us, come on!" They're like a party in a park—anyone can walk up and join, really, because there are no doors or walls.

But other friendship groups are *closed* and un-welcoming to new people. Their attitude is, "Of course you want to hang with us, but you can't be-cause we don't want you!" They're like a party in a locked room with a security guard at the door and a pit bull tied up out front. These closed friendship groups are what we call "cliques."

Here are a couple of helpful words and ideas: When a group wants to be open to others, they're considered *inclusive* because they "include" people. But when they're not open to others, they're *ex-clusive* because they "exclude" people. Friendship groups can be either inclusive or exclusive, but cliques are usually exclusive.

Okay. Now that we're clear on what a clique is, let's talk about them for a bit.

First, it's normal to want a group of special friends to hang with. In fact, it's not only normal, but it's also good. Remember, God made us for community. (Check out the very first chapter, "God's Design.")

Second, it's normal and okay to have some friends who are really special to you (like, your "best friends"). Jesus also had these. He had 12 disciples who were like his friendship group, but three of these guys were his closest friends.

Finally, the problem only comes up when a friendship group becomes a clique. Cliques aren't good for *anyone*—not for the people who are in them, nor for the people who *wish* they were in them. That's why God doesn't like cliques—exclusive groups hurt people, even those who are a part of them.

So just remember that your middle school years will be so much better if you try to be part of inclusive and open friendship groups.

POPULARITY

What does "being popular" mean to you? Is it having lots of friends, being part of the "in" crowd, having the huge house or the "cool" parents, or having a boyfriend or girlfriend? Popularity looks different for everybody, but just about everybody wishes they had a little more of it.

Who *doesn't* want to be known, accepted, and loved by people their own age? Let's take a look at some realities of popularity and what it can mean for you.

Keep it real. There's nothing wrong with being popular. Being friends with lots of people can be an awesome thing. But be careful. Don't try to be popular at the expense of being yourself—the person God made you to be. Don't let popularity change you; and more importantly, don't let your desire to be popular cause you to change how you act and treat your friends. We know lots of people who tried creating a new "them" to be more popular. Most of the time, they eventually discovered they liked the old "them" a whole lot more, and so did everybody else.

Represent. If you consider yourself popular, remember that people are watching you. Actually, believe it or not, people are watching you even if you're *not* popular. What do these people see? Do they see just another middle school student who's part of the in-crowd? Or, do they see somebody who hasn't let her popularity go to her head? Being popular and being a Christian can be a tough combination. But it's also a really cool chance to represent Jesus Christ well.

Put it in perspective. Popularity is way overrated. Joy in life doesn't depend on how popular you are. Look at the many movie stars and professional athletes who are super popular but still feel incredibly lonely. Why? They have it all twisted around. They don't realize (or they've forgotten) that life is not about being known by others. It's about being known by God. Remember, God loves everyone, and he wants you to do the same. Living out this truth as you experience this wacky thing called "middle school" will win you the popularity contest every time.

SHOULD YOU HAVE LOTS OF FRIENDS OR JUST A COUPLE?

We really can't answer this question for you because the answer is different for everybody. Not only that, but just about everyone goes through times in their lives when they have lots of friends and times when they have only a few.

Both of us (Marko and Kurt) have a few people we'd call "core friends," a few more we'd call "close friends," and a whole lot of people who are our casual friends. We'll talk more about these "circles" of friendship in chapter 7, "Understanding the Circles of Friendship."

Usually (although this isn't always true), girls tend to have lots of friends they're sorta close to, while guys tend to have just a couple of friends they're really close to. Girls are more likely to bounce in and out of friendships and to have several "best friends" throughout middle school, while guys are more likely to stick with the same crew over a longer period of time.

When it comes to friendships, maybe it's better to think about quality instead of quantity. In other words, instead of asking, *How* many *friends do I have?* you may want to ask, *How* good *are the friendships I have?*

In fact, that's what this book is all about. We aren't going to talk much about the secrets to having more friends, but we are going to talk a lot about how to make your friendships stronger and healthier. As you thumb through the pages of this book, we'll share about things you can look for in a friend and ways you can be a better friend yourself.

Figuring out this friendship thing is a lifelong journey. You won't completely understand it just because you read this book; but it may help you, and we're glad you're reading it.

"I'VE ONLY GOT TWO PEOPLE I WOULD CALL FRIENDS...
BUT THEY'RE REALLY GOOD ONES."

—RACHEL, 7TH GRADE

FRIENDSHIP AND GENDER

Take a second to think through what you like about your friends. Girls, we bet you can easily think of at least 53 things. Guys, you can probably think of at least three things. Girls and guys naturally look at their friendships differently, and they also have different expectations for their friends (for the most part). Let's take a deeper look at some of the ways friendships work among guys and girls.

GUYS:

You're more likely to look for friends who share your interests and hobbies. Most of the time you spend hanging out with your buddies doesn't require any talking. Actually, most of you would prefer not to talk at all. Your idea of a perfect afternoon with a friend might be to pop some popcorn, grab a Red Bull (or four), and then sit in front of the TV and battle it out in an intense video game session. Or it may mean hanging out at the skate park or starting up a game of street football. What a perfect way to spend a day with a friend or two or three. And you can do all that stuff without having to talk. Grunt, yes. Talk, not so much.

Sure, there are times when you'll talk about deeper stuff, and oftentimes those discussions will lead to an argument of some kind. Every now and then you might get upset and yell at each other, and maybe you'll even throw a punch or two. But for guys, that stuff is no big deal; it's all part of being friends.

GIRLS:

Your friends are your life! You do everything together. You talk all the time about everything and everybody. You talk about the cute guy you sit next to in math class, the latest fashions, the new girl at school, and so on and so on and so on. When you're together, you can laugh hysterically one minute, while in the very next minute you may cry your eyes out. You can talk your friend's ear off, but at the same time you're able to listen to everything she has to say. You give advice, talk on the phone for hours, write notes back and forth in class, and remember each other's birthdays by giving a cute cluster of foil balloons with a bouquet of flowers. You're BFF (best friends forever), and you do all you can to K.I.T. (keep in touch).

Like the boys, there are also times when you'll disagree with your friends. And when girls argue about something, watch out! It can get ugly. Guys usually get over their disagreements quickly; but girls sometimes hold onto them for days, months, even years.

Guys and girls may experience their friendships differently, but ultimately they're both looking for the same thing: To be accepted and loved by someone with whom they can journey down life's road.

UNDERSTANDING THE CIRCLES OF FRIENDSHIP

This chapter is going to require you to do a little writing, so go grab a pencil. We'll wait.

Okay, are you ready? Take a look at those circles at the bottom of the next page. Those are what we call the "circles of friendship." All your friends fit somewhere inside those circles.

The biggest, or outside, ring is your circle of casual friends. Casual friends are people you hang out with at school, at youth group, or on your sports teams, but you probably don't do much with them outside of those settings. Take a few minutes and think of some of your casual friends. Write their names in the outside circle.

The next ring is your circle of close friends. You consider these people your pretty good friends—the ones you hang out with after school, go to the movies with, and maybe even sleep over at each other's houses. Who are your close friends? Write their names in the second circle.

The third and smallest ring is your circle of core friends. Core friendships are the closest and most important to you. These are the friends you really trust, the friends with whom you spend most of your time. Your core friends are probably your very best friends. You may have just one core friend, and that's okay. Write the name(s) of your core friend(s) in that third circle.

It's important to understand that the closer you allow a friend to become, the more influence they'll have in your life. In other words, your core friends have way more influence than your casual friends do. That's an okay thing, as long as the right people are in your "core friends" circle. Allowing the wrong people to become your core friends can cause you all sorts of problems.

You may have noticed there's more space to write in the outer, or "casual friends," ring than in the "close friends" ring. There's also more room to write the names of your close friends than there is to write the names of your core friends. That's true with the circles in this diagram, and it's also true in real life. Because casual friendships don't take as much time and energy, you can have more of them. But healthy core friendships take lots of time and energy, so it's likely you'll have fewer of these.

Okay, you can put away your pencil now.

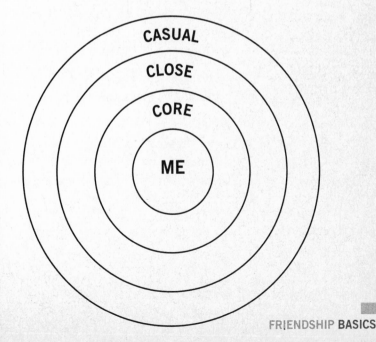

THE POWER OF FRIENDSHIPS

There are tons of reasons why we all need friends. The people we choose to connect with are crucial because we spend so much time with them while attending school and church, playing sports, talking on the phone, instant messaging, hanging out in our free time, and so on.

In Ecclesiastes 4:12 (New Living Translation) it says, "A person standing alone can be attacked and defeated, but two can stand back-to-back and conquer. Three are even better, for a triple-braided cord is not easily broken."

Have you ever tried to break a piece of yarn? It's super easy. How about two pieces at one time? Oh, it's a little more difficult. How about three pieces at a time? That's a lot tougher. Our lives are like pieces of yarn. Standing alone, we're easily broken and defeated; but with one or two close friends beside us, we're stronger—a lot stronger!

Let's take a look at a few reasons why friendships are powerful and how we can be stronger because of them.

My friends know my weaknesses. Not everyone on a team is good at doing the same things. So the only way for the team to be strong is to know each other's weaknesses. In life, when your friends know your weaknesses, they can make you stronger. They can look out for you, help you when you're struggling, and hold you accountable.

My friends share some of the same goals. Have you ever watched a good sports film like *Remember the Titans* or *Hoosiers?* In order to be a successful team, everyone on the team has to share the same goal. In life, what's your goal? Being a good person? Respecting those around you? Following Jesus? It's wise to have friends who share some of your goals because then you can help each other achieve them.

My friends watch my back. Luckily, none of you has had to fight in a real war. Well, maybe you've been in a snowball war, but that's not what we're talking about. In real war situations, soldiers never walk alone. They travel in groups so they can see the enemy from any direction. In life, we're also in a battle. Our enemy, the devil, really wants to mess things up for us, so he comes at us from different directions and in different situations. We want friends who will look out for us and protect us—not just physically, but spiritually, too.

Don't underestimate the power of good friends.

"THE BEST PART ABOUT HAVING FRIENDS IS THAT YOU KNOW
YOU'RE NEVER ON YOUR OWN."

—MARIAH, 7TH GRADE

FRIENDSHIP ADVICE FROM PROVERBS

PROVERBS 27:6

The book of Proverbs in the Bible is full of really cool bits of wisdom. A guy named Solomon, who the Bible says was the wisest man who ever lived, wrote the book of Proverbs. Reading through it is kinda like cracking open a bunch of Christian fortune cookies.

Proverbs has a lot to say about friendship, and we've picked five of our favorite little pieces of advice and wisdom.

"WOUNDS FROM A SINCERE FRIEND ARE BETTER THAN MANY KISSES FROM AN ENEMY" (PROVERBS 27:6, NLT)

That's an interesting verse, isn't it? But when you stop to think about it, it makes a ton of sense. Another way to say this might be: "A good friend tells you what you *need* to hear, while someone who doesn't really care about you tells you what you *want* to hear."

Let's put this in a real-life setting: You start hanging around a rougher group of kids, and you're beginning to change the way you act in order to fit in. The more you change, the more your new friends cheer you on and the more they seem to like you. You know you're not behaving the way you should, but you really like all the attention you're getting.

Meanwhile, one of your core friends—somebody you've known for a long time—has noticed you're acting way different. One day this friend pulls you aside and tells you you've been acting like a jerk and you need to straighten out. Chances are good that the conversation would hurt you a bit. After all, nobody likes to be called out by a friend.

This verse in Proverbs is saying there are true friends and there are those people who only *act* like friends. A true friend looks out for you and wants the best for you—even when it hurts. A true friend doesn't purposely say and do mean things to you, but also isn't afraid to wound you a little bit to help keep you on the right track.

PROVERBS 12:26

"THE RIGHTEOUS CHOOSE THEIR FRIENDS CAREFULLY, BUT THE WAY OF THE WICKED LEADS THEM ASTRAY" (PROVERBS 12:26, TODAY'S NEW INTERNATIONAL VERSION)

The book of Proverbs is packed full of all kinds of good advice. And this verse has some HUGE advice about friends. Can you tell what it says? Here's how another Bible translation says it:

"GODLY PEOPLE ARE CAREFUL ABOUT THE FRIENDS THEY CHOOSE. BUT THE WAY OF SINNERS LEADS THEM DOWN THE WRONG PATH." (NEW INTERNATIONAL READER'S VERSION)

See? The advice is pretty clear, really. The writer of Proverbs is saying, "Don't be stupid. Pick your friends carefully." (By the way, have you ever heard this saying: "You can pick your friends, and you can pick your nose, but you can't pick your friend's nose"? No, that's not from the Bible.)

But *why* does the Bible say we should pick our friends carefully? The answer is right there in the verse. Your friends—the people you hang out with and spend time with—have a *huge* impact on your life, whether or not you want them to, are aware of it, or care.

That doesn't mean you have to have friends who are exactly like you in every way. And it *certainly* doesn't mean you should have only Christian friends. It just means you have to be wise. You have to be careful. You have to ask yourself, *How are my friends influencing me? Is this how I want to be influenced?*

PROVERBS 17:9

News Flash: There's no such thing as a "perfect friendship." The reason why there are no perfect friendships is because friendships involve people, and there are no perfect people. You may have perfect hair, or you may get a perfect score on your math test, but *you* aren't perfect.

God knows that even among good friends some stuff will happen that shouldn't. Purposely hurtful things will be said and selfishness, gossip, and jealousy will creep in. Sometimes it'll be your fault, and sometimes it'll be the fault of your friends. But no matter who's at fault, when stuff goes bad in a friendship, you have a choice. This verse in Proverbs lays it out for you:

"LOVE PROSPERS WHEN A FAULT IS FORGIVEN, BUT DWELLING ON IT SEPARATES CLOSE FRIENDS" (PROVERBS 17:9, NLT)

When you choose to forgive, you're allowing your friendship to grow and get better. In a really cool way, a friendship that's gone through some tough times can be better than ever if forgiveness has been offered and accepted.

But when you choose *not* to forgive, or you choose to hold a grudge, you're allowing whatever happened to separate you from your friend. The Bible uses the phrase "dwelling on it" because it means you refuse to let it go. "Dwelling on it" means you don't forgive the person and you bring up their mistake over and over again. "Dwelling on it" means that even though your friend said he's sorry, you keep reminding him of that time he chucked the Xbox controller across the room—or whatever it was he did.

You aren't perfect and neither are your friends. If you're like most middle schoolers, your friends have done some dumb stuff to you. And most kids will choose to dwell on those things and let them chip away at the friendship. But you can be different. You can choose to forgive your friend; and when you do, you'll be surprised how much your friendship grows.

PROVERBS 17:17

If you were to ask a bunch of people what qualities they want their friends to have, one word would be near the top of just about everybody's list: loyalty. People want loyalty to be part of their friendships. Guess what? God does, too.

"A FRIEND IS ALWAYS LOYAL, AND A BROTHER IS BORN TO HELP IN TIME OF NEED" (PROVERBS 17:17, NLT)

Being loyal basically means being faithful to your friends. It means being committed to them. Loyalty in a friendship means you stick by each other in good times and in bad times. Sounds easy, right? You've probably already learned that creating a sense of loyalty with your friends is almost never easy. Here's why:

Loyalty takes time. Developing a real sense of loyalty among friends doesn't happen overnight. Loyalty is developed over time.

Loyalty is misunderstood. This is a biggie! Being a loyal friend means being faithful and committed, which sometimes means calling her out when she's making poor choices or when she's getting involved in stuff that can hurt her or others. Lots and lots of middle school students know their friends are in trouble, but they don't do anything about it because they believe they'd be betraying their friends to do so. Sometimes being loyal to a friend means speaking up—even when your friend doesn't want to hear it, and even when she mistakes your loyalty for betrayal. (Remember Proverbs

27:6?) Please hear us on this one. Being loyal doesn't mean being a tattletale every time your friend does something wrong, but it does mean being willing to confront your friend and asking an adult for help if your friend's behavior is dangerous.

Loyalty gets put to the test—a lot. Your friend will mess up. You'll mess up. Your friend will say something that hurts your feelings. You'll say something that hurts your friend's feelings. The list of little things that can chip away at your friendships is a long one. However, loyalty is a two-way street. As your friendship grows, your friend will do fewer things that might hurt the friendship, and you'll be quicker to forgive her when she does. You'll also do fewer things to hurt the friendship, and your friend will be quicker to forgive you as well.

Loyalty is a huge part of a healthy friendship. Expect it from your friends. More importantly, expect it from yourself.

PROVERBS 27:17

One of the neat things about the Bible is the way God uses word-pictures or images to help us understand what he's talking about. The short little verse below gives us a picture of something God thinks is really important in a friendship.

"AS IRON SHARPENS IRON, SO A FRIEND SHARPENS A FRIEND"
(PROVERBS 27:17, NLT)

Have you ever thought about what life would be like without knives? How would butter be spread on a piece of bread? How would that fresh fish you caught be gutted and cleaned? How would you cut up that huge, juicy pork chop you can't wait to bite into? What would your grandpa use to whittle a stick? A knifeless life would make everyday tasks a lot tougher.

Sometimes having a *dull* knife can be worse than having no knife. A dull knife does you no good, especially when you're trying to cut into a steak. You might feel like the knife let you down. It can be super disappointing and frustrating.

This verse in Proverbs is saying that knives and friendship have a couple things in common: They both need to be sharpened, and they use each other for the sharpening process. People sharpened iron (which is the kind of metal knives were made from back in Bible times) with another piece of iron, scraping the two pieces together until the dull piece (the knife) was sharp.

God compares this concept of knife sharpening to our relationships with our friends. He wants us to be the kinds of friends who make our friends stronger or sharper. He encourages us to help sharpen them so they're better able to do what God has created them to do.

A good friendship is one in which the friends sharpen each other and lift each other up. A poor friendship is one in which the friends dull each other and pull each other down.

Life without good, sharp knives would be no fun. Life without good, sharp friendships would be even worse. Are your friendships cutting it?

I WAS A MIDDLE SCHOOL DORK!
—KURT

It started out like any other Friday night in sixth grade. I was spending the night at Mike Pace's house, his parents were out with friends, and we were bored. As we sat around his house looking for something to do, his older brother, John, hollered for us to come into the kitchen. Above the stove in a hard-to-reach cabinet was an old oil lantern. Next to the lantern was a can of fuel oil—highly flammable oil.

Mistake #1: We thought it would be fun to fill the lamp with oil and light it, so John grabbed a stepstool and pulled the lantern and oil down from the cabinet where they'd been safely stored for years.

Mistake #2: We excitedly unscrewed the top of the lantern and filled it to overflowing with oil. We *literally* filled it to overflowing and nervously giggled as we watched oil pour out of the top of the lantern and onto the stove.

Mistake #3: We lit the lantern anyway. But since there was oil all over the lantern and the stove, we didn't light just the lantern—we also lit the top of the stove.

Mistake #4: Panicking while we watched the entire lantern and stovetop go up in flames. I somehow thought it was a good idea to knock the lantern off the stove, which I did. As soon as the lantern hit the floor, it shattered and oil spread throughout the kitchen. Burning oil!

Mistake #5: Mike ran out to the back yard, dipped a huge bucket into his swimming pool, ran back into the house, and threw the water on the oily fire. We suddenly learned what you may already know: Oil and water don't mix. Instead of putting the fire out, the water only spread the fire more because the oil floated on top of the water and the flames went everywhere the water went.

The three of us stood there in shock as we watched the flames spread from the kitchen into the dining room. Finally John, who was much older and wiser (he was in ninth grade), had an idea. He grabbed several blankets, dipped them into the pool, and then tossed them on top of the flames, smothering them.

Mistake #6: After cleaning up the mess, we noticed some burn marks on a couple walls. Most kids would have been smart enough to simply leave things as they were and just tell their parents what happened. After all, it was an honest mistake. A BIG mistake, but still an honest one. Unfortunately, we weren't very smart. We decided to try to paint the entire kitchen before Mike and John's parents got home!

Somehow, we thought his parents wouldn't notice the smell of fresh paint. Like I said, we weren't very smart.

BIBLICAL FRIENDSHIPS

JONATHAN AND DAVID

There are all kinds of friendships in the Bible—in both the Old and New Testaments—that we can study and learn from now. You'll notice that the friendships in the Bible are much like our friendships today. They all had their share of ups, and they also had plenty of downs. As we dig into these biblical friendships, think about your own friends and ask yourself, *Do I have a friendship that reflects this one? If not, is there someone I know who could possibly be this kind of friend?*

As you read about the friendship of Jonathan and David, you can sense the deep ties they have with each other. It wasn't a friendship that developed overnight but over a ton of time spent together. There are many things we can learn from Jon and Dave, but there is one quality that seems to stick out above the rest: sacrifice.

For most middle schoolers, sacrificing for a friend means giving her one of your Twinkies at lunch. But these guys understood what sacrifice in a friendship was all about. So let's take a quick look at the sacrifices they made for each other.

Time. Time is a fragile thing. You probably already feel too busy and like you don't have time for all the stuff you need to do. As you get older, you'll probably feel like you have even less time. When you look at David and Jonathan's friendship, you can see that even though life was busy for both of them, they made sacrifices to spend time with each other. As a result, their friendship was really strong.

Energy. Jonathan and David's friendship also shows a sacrifice of energy. Even after a long, tiring day, they stretched themselves to have the energy to counsel, encourage, and pray for each other. It's easy to say you're too tired to talk, listen, or hang out, but a sacrificial friendship needs a little extra energy, even if you think it's not there.

Humility. Jonathan and David were both humble enough to put their friend's needs above their own. They sacrificed by considering their friend more important than themselves. At one point Jonathan said David could count on him to do anything that David needed (1 Samuel 20:4).

Jonathan and David had a give-and-take friendship. In other words, they both sacrificed for the other. It wasn't a one-sided deal, but a very healthy balance. A balance of sacrifice we all should strive for in our friendships.

SHADRACH, MESHACH, AND ABEDNEGO

These three friends, whose story is in the Old Testament book of Daniel (you TOTALLY have to read it—it's fantastic!) went through some seriously tough stuff together. And they were probably teenagers at the time.

First, they were taken 900 miles away from their families and homes and put into a kind of boarding school that was run by a king who wanted to brainwash their religion right out of them. Even their names were changed. Shadrach (SHAD-rack) used to be Hananiah; Meshach (ME-shack) used to be Mishael; and Abednego (a-BED-nee-go) used to be Azariah.

Once they were living in this new "school," they were expected to give up all their beliefs about God. In fact, the king (who'd personally thought up the brainwashing boarding school) ordered the royal statue makers to create a giant gold statue of himself. And then he ordered everyone in the kingdom (including the dudes at the boarding school, of course) to bow down and worship it. Wow! This guy had issues! Oh, and to make it even worse, the king said anyone who *wouldn't* bow down to the statue would be thrown into a massively hot furnace. Crispy-critter time.

Well, Shad, Shaq, and Bed wouldn't do it. They wouldn't bow down to the big statue of the king. WHAT MASSIVE COURAGE! Seriously! These teenage guys knew the consequences of what they were saying. In fact, once they were tied up and about to be tossed into the furnace, they said, "If we are thrown into the blazing furnace, the God we serve is able to save us from it, and he will rescue us from your hand, O king. But even if he does not, we want you to know, O king, that we will not serve your gods or worship the image of gold you have set up" (Daniel 3:17-18).

Do you have friends like that? Do you have friends who give you strength and courage to live for God? Man, we're tellin' ya—those are the best kinds of friends to have in life.

DAVID'S MIGHTY MEN
(THE WATER BOYS)

Check out this story from 2 Samuel 23:

> During harvest time, three of the thirty chief warriors came down to David at the cave of Adullam, while a band of Philistines was encamped in the Valley of Rephaim. At that time David was in the stronghold, and the Philistine garrison was at Bethlehem. David longed for water and said, "Oh, that someone would get me a drink of water from the well near the gate of Bethlehem!" So the three mighty warriors broke through the Philistine lines, drew water from the well near the gate of Bethlehem and carried it back to David... Such were the exploits of the three mighty warriors. (vv. 13-17)

David and all his fighting dudes were camped out in a cave, trying to avoid a major battle. And the cave was really well protected, so they were pretty safe. But they were also massively bored. And big-time homesick. One night they're chillin' around a fire, telling stories or something, and David shows his homesickness by mentioning how much he'd love some of that great-tasting water from that well near his home in the city.

Of course, there's almost no way to *get* water from that well because the enemy army is camped in the valley between the cave and the well. And to make it even worse, the leaders of the enemy army are camped *right inside* the city with the well.

But three guys decide it would be really cool to get David a drink of that water. So later that night, they sneak through the sleeping enemy camp and right up to the well. They get some water and sneak all the way back to the cave. They *easily* could have been caught and killed.

Do you have friends who encourage you to do things for God that seem a bit crazy? Like, do you have friends who encourage you to tell the truth? Or to say "no" to stuff that doesn't honor God? Or to let people know about Jesus? Doing that kind of stuff—stuff that's so hard to do it almost feels crazy to try—is sure easier (and more fun) when you have friends who want to stand with you. Get some friends who are *crazy* for God.

PAUL AND BARNABAS

One of the toughest parts about being a Christian in middle school is trying to actually live in a way that makes others want to know about Jesus. We know we should tell others about God's love for them, but it's just so scary.

Paul and Barnabas had a very unique friendship, and telling others about church and Jesus Christ was something they did together quite a bit. As Christians with a huge desire to reach those who didn't have a personal relationship with Christ, they told people about the good news of Jesus almost every day. They were a great two-man team.

These guys worked very well together and were super-successful at reaching a common goal. They complemented each other—where one was weak, the other was strong. If there were such a thing as a sport of "people-reaching," then Paul and Barnabas would be a dynasty, like the Los Angeles Lakers of the 1980s and the New England Patriots of the 2000s. They traveled from town to town on their camels (or donkeys), and together they presented the awesome story of Jesus in a real and relevant way to thousands of people.

It wasn't all fine and dandy every time Paul and Barnabas hit the road. (One time they had a huge disagreement that hurt their friendship for a while.) But their common desire to share God's love bonded them in a special way. Think about how much tougher it would have been if either one tried to do this incredible task alone. They weren't always together while they told people about Jesus, but they knew they weren't alone, either. They both knew their buddy was busy doing the same thing somewhere else.

What if you and one of your friends decided it was time to start telling other people about God's love and about his Son, Jesus? Yes, it would be scary. Yes, it would be risky. But what an experience!

Barnabas and Paul's friendship made a difference in the world around them. Your friendships can make a difference, too.

THE DISCIPLES

Have you ever wondered what it would've been like to be one of Jesus' 12 disciples? Jesus' 12 closest friends spent time talking to him, laughing with him, teaching with him, standing next to him as he performed amazing miracles, sitting around the campfire roasting marshmallows (or figs), and just asking him for advice about life. They spent hours and hours together every day for about three years.

Jesus chose 12 ordinary men to teach, train, and mentor about the things of God and his plan for mankind. He did this to prepare his disciples for what he wanted them to do after he finished his ministry on earth. Sprinkled among all the fun times with Jesus, the disciples had their share of insecurities, doubts, and pressures to do what's right. They also disagreed with each other at times and allowed jealousy and greed to creep into their friendships.

We actually see some of this take place in Mark 9:33-35:

> After they arrived at Capernaum and settled in a house, Jesus asked his disciples, "What were you discussing out on the road?" But they didn't answer, because they had been arguing about which of them was the greatest. He sat down, called the twelve disciples over to him, and said, "Whoever wants to be first must take last place and be the servant of everyone else." (NLT)

We can see that the disciples spent some time arguing and comparing themselves to each other. They squabbled about which one was the greatest disciple, and they asked themselves questions like, *Who's closest to Jesus? Who's taught in front of the largest crowd? Who takes charge when Jesus isn't around? Who's the smartest among us? Who rides shotgun next to Jesus on the camel most often?* The verses you just read show how Jesus put the disciples in their place and put it all in perspective.

What happened among the disciples is something we can learn from as we look at our own friendships. Jesus doesn't want us to compare ourselves to others because it invites jealousy to enter our friendships. Don't look at what your friend has that you don't have. Instead, look at what you *do* have and think about how you can use it to strengthen your friendship.

Take it from Jesus: In order to be the best possible friend, the first thing you need is the ability to be last—to be a servant to everybody else.

Nothing compares to that kind of friend.

JOB'S FRIENDS

Do you know the story of Job (JOBE)? It's a trippy one. Job was this amazing dude who loved God and was big-time righteous (meaning, he did right things). One day, Satan was talking smack to God about how no humans would ever stay true to God if their lives were bad enough, and God said that wouldn't be the case with Job. So Satan goes off on Job to see if he can get Job to turn his back on God. Job loses everything: his wealth, his fields, his home, his kids, even his own health.

Then Job's friends show up—three of 'em. They do one really great thing, and then they do some really stupid things. Let's talk about the great thing they did first.

Job is in massive pain (physically, yes, but even more so emotionally). He's sitting in the dirt, probably crying, and certainly feeling very, very sad. And he's not saying anything; he's just sad. Then his friends come and sit with him. They don't say anything for—ready for this?—days! *Really.* They sit with him in silence for days. Isn't that cool? They knew his pain was very, very deep and the last thing he needed was a whole bunch of talking.

When your friend is hurting, she might want to talk. But more often, it's just good to have someone sit there with you and *not* talk.

But then Job's friends go stupid. They start giving him lame advice. They tell him his life must be a mess because of something he did. Now, for sure, sometimes our lives *are* a mess because of things we do. However, this isn't the case with Job, and he keeps trying to tell his friends that. But they won't let it go; they keep telling him he must have sinned.

If your friend is really hurting, it *might* be because of some lame choices she made, right? But often, our friends are hurting—like Job—because bad things have happened to them. Don't make it worse by being like Job's friends.

JESUS' FRIENDSHIP WITH PETER

Peter was one of Jesus' 12 disciples. The Bible tells us Jesus loved Peter very much. They were friends who shared life together, respected each other, and knew each other really well. At times they didn't even have to say anything to communicate with each other—just a look said it all. Kind of like when your mom gives you "the look," which tells you she's very upset about something.

Peter showed his love and devotion for Jesus on a regular basis. Peter stood firm in his passion and desire to follow Jesus. Peter had such a solid belief and conviction in who Jesus was that Jesus even gave Peter a nickname—"the rock" (Matthew 16:17-18).

But Peter's strong devotion to Jesus weakened. He actually went so far as to deny he knew Jesus at all (Matthew 26:69-75). At the moment Jesus needed Peter most, "the rock" crumbled and wasn't there to support him. When the going got tough, Peter got going—in the opposite direction! Peter fled the scene and left his friend behind. Don't be too hard on old Pete, though, because you probably would have done the same thing. After all, Jesus was in pretty big trouble, and Peter was scared to death. Later on, Peter recognized he'd made a huge mistake, Jesus forgave him, and Peter ended up closer to Jesus than ever before. In fact, Peter became one of the greatest leaders of the Christian movement.

Since none of your friends are being wrongly arrested and sentenced to death (at least we hope they aren't), it should be a little easier for you to stand by their side when they're going through tough times.

Are you someone who sticks up for your friends? Do you have your friends' backs no matter what the situation? One mark of a true friendship is being willing to stick next to each other through thick and thin.

Jesus and Peter were about as close as friends can get, and they still had their issues. You and your closest friends are going to have your issues, too. But tough times don't have to ruin friendships. In fact, just as they did with Peter, tough times can actually make you a better friend.

JESUS' FRIENDSHIP WITH MARY

Mary was Jesus' mother. She gave birth to him, raised him, taught him to do what's right (although since Jesus is God, she didn't need to do that), put food on his table, taught him how to tie his sandals, and reminded him to do his chores. Jesus loved his mom. They had a very close mother-son relationship. In fact, they had a friendship. Here are some practical ways you can deepen and strengthen your friendship with your mom, too.

Talk with her. Duh! Talking to each other is a pretty important part of any friendship. It's an important part of your friendship with your mom, too. There are lots of middle school students (especially boys) who don't really talk to their moms. They might say something to her, but it's usually no more that one or two words at a time. In order to develop a deeper friendship with your mom, you need to have a conversation with her. Answer her questions (with complete sentences), and ask her a question every now and again. Share with her what's going on at school and at church. Tell her you love her, even if she knows it by your actions. Try this stuff! Warning: The act of talking to your mom may cause her to faint right in front of your eyes.

Hug her. Sometimes actions speak louder than words. And a simple hug can speak volumes. It can say "thank you" or "I love you." When you were younger, your mom would give you hugs all the time, even when you couldn't hug her back. As you've gotten a little older, she may not be sure when you want a hug and when you don't. So make the first move. And make hugging your mom an every-day thing. She's your mom! It's the least you can do.

Respect her. Jesus respected his mom. Respect is simply showing your mom you love her by obeying her. This is so important that God made it one of the Ten Commandments. Doing what your mom says (and when she says it) not only shows her that you respect her authority, but it also shows her that you can handle responsibility. And with more responsibility comes more freedom. Every middle school student wants some free-dom. Here's the deal: Jesus was perfect, yet he still chose to respect his mom and her authority. So you can do the same.

You gotta remember that your mom is human. She's made mistakes in the past (so have you), and she'll make more mistakes in the future (so will you). Love her for who she is and thank her for what she's done for you, because no matter how much life changes, she'll always be your mom.

BEST FRIENDS

There are all kinds of friends, right? I mean, you might consider some kid from school you've talked to only three times in your whole life as being your friend. But that's clearly not the same kind of relationship as the one you have with someone you've been best friends with for six years.

And that's okay. Jesus had friendships of different intensities also. There was a large group of people he hung around with all the time. These were his friends. Then there were the 12 disciples to whom he was much closer. They were his main friendship group. And then there were three disciples (Peter, James, and John) who were Jesus' closest friends. And from what we read in the Bible, it seems John was probably Jesus' *best* friend. (Maybe they each wore little "best friends forever" necklaces or something.)

So you might have a best friend. Or you might not. Girls make a bigger deal out of this than guys do (in general, that is). Lots of middle school girls seem to think it's pretty important to have a best friend. Guys might also have a best friend, but they don't seem to think it's as important to say so.

But here's the deal: It's likely that your friendships will change a lot during middle school, and this is super-normal (see chapter 2, "Shifting Friendships"). But there are a few ways the best-friend thing can be not so good.

First, it's not good to think about it all the time. You know how a little puppy pants really quickly? Some middle schoolers act that way about having a best friend: "Who's my best friend?" "Are you my best friend?" "I need a best friend." "Will you be my best friend?" Strangely, this kind of urgent push for a best friend can actually *prevent* you from making friends—because it's annoying!

Second, some middle schoolers change best friends (especially girls) like they change their clothes. And this constant changing and claiming and dumping and shifting *almost always* results in people getting hurt. It's not worth it. Just enjoy the friends you have and don't be so concerned about who is whose *best* friend.

And, finally, best friends are great when they bring a sense of deep commitment and closeness. But when that means you can't be friends with other people—or when the two of you won't include others—well, that's when best friendships end up hurting everyone.

NON-ROMANTIC, OPPOSITE-GENDER FRIENDS

When you were a little kid, it probably didn't seem weird at all to have friends of the opposite sex. (Like, if you're a girl, to have a friend who's a guy; or if you're a guy, to have a friend who's a girl.) You played together and everything seemed normal. Perhaps you even talked about getting married someday—but it didn't mean anything. It's not like you were "dating" or something.

But when you're in middle school, having friends of the opposite sex can start to feel a little weird. Or, even if it still feels totally normal to you, people might give you a hard time about the friendship. Either way, you'll probably notice it's different than when you were a kid.

My daughter, Liesl, is in middle school (this is Marko writing), and right now she has a really close friend who's a guy. But they're not girlfriend and boyfriend at all! In fact, my daughter *has* a boyfriend, and it's not this guy. Yet people are always asking them, "You two like each other, don't you?" So Liesl says, "Well, yeah, we like each other as friends. Don't you *like* your friends?"

Here's what we (Marko and Kurt) want you to know: It's *great* to have friends of the opposite sex. And it's *wonderful* to have them and never think about becoming "romantic" with them. We can learn so much from the opposite sex because there *are* differences between girls and guys (and not just physical ones either), and these can result in different kinds of friendships that are really special and good.

So don't allow other people, or TV shows, or magazines, or music, or your parents, or anything or anyone else try to convince you that if you have a friend of the opposite sex, it has to be romantic. That's just stupid. And if you can learn now, while you're in middle school, to have opposite-sex friendships that aren't all weird and "possibly romantic," that's a skill and a value that will be great to have for the rest of your life.

TYPICAL GIRL FRIENDSHIP GROUPS

It's always a bit dangerous to define people and say, "This is what most girls are like," or "This is what most guys are like," or "This is what most middle schoolers are like." There are always exceptions. In this chapter and the next, we're going to describe what most girl friendships and what most guy friendships are like in middle school. You might not fit these descriptions—and that is *totally* fine. We're writing these chapters so you can better understand yourself, as well as your friends.

Most middle school girls have friendship groups of two or three girls. There might be more girls in a wider group of friends, but it's really important to most middle school girls to know who their closest friends are. (This isn't as big a deal to most guys.)

For a bunch of reasons, it seems like friendship groups of four or more girls usually don't last. Instead, they typically split up into smaller groups. Part of the reason for this divide is that girls expect their friendships to have two things—and in very large doses: commitment and closeness. Guys might want those things also, but they really stink at expressing it (in most cases).

So let's start with commitment. Girls want friendships that are super-committed, which means they want friends they can count on. That's why it's really important to girls to *define* who their best friends are. They want it to be very clear: "I'm committed to you, and you're committed to me."

Girls also want closeness. In other words, they want their friendships to be deep where both friends are willing to share secrets, trust each other, and be really honest. This is because it's super-important to girls to be known. Actually, it's important to guys also—but, once again, guys are normally pretty lame at expressing this or even being aware of it.

This is part of the reason why girls often change friends in middle school. Not only are they trying to find friendships that will offer them the deep level of commitment and closeness they're looking for, but also they want friends who are enjoyable to hang out with. It's not an easy combination to find!

TYPICAL GUY FRIENDSHIP GROUPS

Middle school guys seem to have very different friendships than girls do. (Read the previous chapter about girl friendship groups, if you haven't already.) Both middle school guys and girls are going through major changes in their friendships, but it usually looks really different for guys than it does for girls.

Part of the reason for this is that—in general—girls love to talk, and guys don't as much. Check this out: The average teenage guy uses about 4,000 words each day. Sounds like a lot, huh? Well, not so much. Guys, in fact, hardly use any words compared to girls! The average teenage girl uses (are you ready for this?) 20,000 words each day—that's five times as many words as guys use. Wow. That's huge! So, of course girls' friendships are going to be more about talking than guys' friendships are.

Guys grunt more.

No, really! Because middle school guys aren't as good at expressing themselves with words, it can be a major challenge for guys to form friendships. After all, it's hard to become friends with someone if you don't talk. Really. Think about it!

So middle schools guys tend to be at one of two extremes. Lots of middle school guys run in packs, like wild wolves. They usually form friendship groups around a common interest, such as, "we're the guys into skateboarding," or "we're the guys into baseball." Or whatever. These friendship groups can be great, or they can be terrible, or anywhere in between. But they're typically very different from girls' friendship groups.

Then at the other extreme are the guys who don't really have friends. They might have some childhood friends they still see sometimes or maybe that guy from school who came over to play video games once or twice. But they don't have any friends who really know them.

If this is you, we want you to know, first of all, that it doesn't mean you're a freak or unworthy of friendship. In fact, it's very normal. We also want to encourage you to try making some friendships because they're such an important part of our lives. You might consider asking a youth worker at your church or some other adult you trust for some suggestions on how to make friends. Of course, you can also read section 10 of this book. It's all about making friends!

Before we wrap up this chapter, we should also mention that there are lots of guys who fall right in the middle of these two extremes, guys who really *do* have close friendships. If you're one of them—we think that's fantastic.

OTHER TYPES OF FRIENDS

One of the best parts about being young is having friends all over the place. Think about it for a second. You see your school friends just about every day. You see your youth group friends once or twice a week. You hang out with your neighborhood friends after school. You see your sports friends at soccer, football, lacrosse, softball, volleyball, or basketball practices. You see your first and second cousins at Thanksgiving, Christmas, and Easter. In fact, you probably have a bunch of different types of friends we don't even know about. Some of you have scuba-diving friends, Future Farmers of America friends, math club friends, skate park friends, and student council friends. Get the point? Being a middle school kid is an awesome time to have friends from all different parts of life.

As you get older, you'll discover that more of your friends will come from fewer areas of your life. That's not a terrible thing; it's just a different thing. But for now, you probably find yourself in lots of different arenas with lots of different friends. How cool is that!

If that's the case, then you may have already discovered something we're going to look at in more detail in our next chapter: It seems just about each category of friends has its own "code of conduct." How you talk, what you talk about, what you joke about, how you dress, how you treat each other, what music you listen to, and so on are all examples of the code of conduct or the way each group of friends sorta expects each other to behave.

Sometimes it can be tough to remember how to act within the different groups. You certainly don't want to make the mistake of acting like a jock around your math club friends. So what do you do? What's the answer?

We have a suggestion: Keep reading!

COMPARTMENTALIZED FRIENDSHIP GROUPS

We're gonna teach you a big word. Ready? It's *compartmentalized*. Whoa! You probably had to say that really slowly, huh?

Think of a makeup kit or a fishing tackle box. They have lots of little spaces—compartments—for different things. If it's a makeup kit, you put your lipstick in one compartment, your eye shadow in another compartment, and your, um, tweezers (we don't really know—we're guys!) into a third compartment. (Don't girls use tweezers for something?) If it's a tackle box, you put your lures in one compartment, your bobbers in another, and your uh...um...extra fishing line (yeah!) in yet another compartment. (We'll be honest—neither of us goes fishing any more than we put on makeup.)

The point of the compartments is to keep everything separate.

Some people—middle schoolers included—do that with their lives. It's called "compartmentalization."

Lots of middle school kids—especially middle school kids who go to church—compartmentalize their friends. They have a church group of friends and a school group of friends. And they try to keep the two groups separate (compartmentalized) so it's easier for them to act one way with the first group and a different way with the second group.

So with your church friends, you might be all Jesus-y and watch your language and stuff like that. And you might even mean it. But with your school friends, you might curse like a sailor and do all kinds of other stuff that you'd *never* do in front of your church friends.

This compartmentalization thing is not good. In fact, it's a pretty lousy way to live. God wants you to live a life that's whole and honest. God wants you to be you—the "you" he made you to be. You're ripping yourself off when you compartmentalize your friends (and your life) like that. It teaches you to live like an actor all the time, just performing the roles you believe your different groups of friends expect you to play. That's not really you.

So bust out of the compartments and be you! (It's okay to keep your makeup or fishing junk in different compartments, though.)

I WAS A MIDDLE SCHOOL DORK!
—MARKO

I once had a teacher named Mrs. Jobbit. Of course, we couldn't resist calling her "Jabba the Hut" (as in the *Return of the Jedi* character). Mrs. Jobbit was one of the nicest teachers I had in middle school. She was funny, and she was a good sport if and when we teased her.

But this time I crossed the line—big time.

I was into practical jokes during that time, and my friends and I really loved a store near my home that sold magic tricks and gag gifts and stuff like that. We thought sneezing powder was the coolest thing, and we'd used it in many of the practical jokes we played on each other and on various family members. I thought it would be *hilarious* to blow sneezing powder into Mrs. Jobbit's face.

My friend Chris and I worked out a plan. He would call Mrs. Jobbit over to his desk, ask her a question, and point at his paper so she would bend down for a better look. Chris sat right in front of me, so this would give me a clear and up-close shot at her face.

Normally, we'd use about a quarter of one packet of sneezing powder. But I wanted to make sure it worked, so I emptied two whole packets into my hand. It looked like a large pile of baking flour.

The plan worked perfectly: Chris called Mrs. Jobbit over, and she bent down to look at his paper. Then I leaned forward, raised my open palm in front of her face, and blew.

It was too much sneezing powder. It was a sneezing-powder overdose.

It stuck to her face, completely covering her in white dust. Mrs. Jobbit quickly stood up with her eyes wide. Immediately—various liquids started flowing out of every opening in her face! Her eyes started to water like crazy, and her makeup was running in little streams. Her nose was also running, like I'd never seen a nose run before. She was probably drooling too, but I don't think I could see at that point—I was in full-blown panic mode. I had that overwhelming sense of, *What was I thinking?*

Mrs. Jobbit said, "Out in the hall. NOW!" So I went and stood in the hall, shaking and afraid. Eventually, Mrs. Jobbit came out and talked to me. She said she could kick me out of school. I cried (seriously). But Mrs. Jobbit had mercy on me and only kept me after school a couple of days. See, she really *was* a nice teacher!

MORE THAN FRIENDS

WHY IS THIS SUDDENLY AN ISSUE?

Oh man. That girl—she's lived a few blocks away from you for years. You always thought she was just a girl who lived a few blocks away from you—nothing more, nothing less. But, suddenly, she's...well... she's so amazing, so interesting, so...um...hot.

That guy in your homeroom? He's always been a dork. And he still is—he does stupid and annoying stuff all the time. But still...he...well, it seems like he got totally cute, like, overnight!

What's the deal with this? Why are you suddenly thinking about other kids *romantically?* (That's a weird word, we know; but you know what we mean.)

This isn't a sex book, so we're not going to start explaining how all of that works. (Some of you are greatly relieved right now, thinking, *Oh, good. I'm glad this isn't a sex book!* And some of you are really bummed right now, thinking, *Oh, man, I wish this were a sex book!)* But we'll tell you why this girl-guy attraction thing seems to have shifted into high gear.

It's your brain's fault. Well, that's not totally true. It's really God's fault (if we're allowed to say that anything is God's "fault"). Let's put it this way: God made you—and your brain—to be this way. Sometime in about sixth or seventh grade, most middle schoolers start—are you ready for the big word that grosses out most middle schoolers?—*puberty*. Ha! You probably cringed when you read that word. Puberty, puberty, puberty. We wish we could see the look on your face right now—but we're guessing you're just thinking, *Stop with that word already!*

Fine. Be that way.

When you go through...um...*that word*, it's the fast lane of change to becoming an adult in every way: the way you think, the way your body is shaped, the way you feel things (like emotions), even the way you believe. Your brain is traveling on the superhighway to adulthood. And part of that journey involves revving up the part of your brain that tells you, "Ooh, she looks good," or "Hey, I think I might kinda like him." That's a good thing: God invented it and put it in you, and God decided this point in your life—your early teenage years—is when it should kick in.

WHY ROMANTIC STUFF CAN RUIN FRIENDSHIPS
(*WITH YOUR OTHER FRIENDS*), PART 1

We've seen it a hundred times. No, we've seen it 200 times. Correction—we've seen it 300 times! The formula goes something like this:

- Boy has friends. Girl has friends.

- Boy and girl like each other.

- Boy and girl decide to become more than just friends.

- Boy starts ignoring his old friends. Girl starts ignoring her old friends.

- Friendships get all messed up.

You think we're exaggerating, don't you? We really aren't, we've seen it happen over and over again. You've probably seen it happen, too. But why does it happen? That's a great question! Here are a few thoughts:

No time for the old friends. A new romance takes time. It means hanging out at lunch, talking on the phone, and begging rides to the mall so you can be together. All this time spent developing a new romance means you're spending less time with your old friends.

Jealousy. Jealousy almost always shows up when middle schoolers begin to get romantic. The old friends are jealous of the new "special friend." And the "special friend" is jealous of the old friends. As a result, both sides start putting extra pressure on you to spend more and more time with them.

Choosing sides. When jealousy sets in, people start forcing you to make a choice. They'll say things like, "You need to choose between your new girlfriend and us," or, "If you want to be my boyfriend, you can't keep hanging out with your buddies." Guess what? Nine times out of 10 the new romance wins out and the friendships lose. We've seen guys and girls walk away from lifelong friends because they think they're in love with somebody they've only known for a little while.

If you decide you want to become "more than just friends" with somebody, you need to do so very carefully. We think there are all kinds of possible problems with having a boyfriend or girlfriend in middle school. What it might do to your relationships with your other friends is just one example.

MY FRIENDS

WHY ROMANTIC STUFF CAN RUIN FRIENDSHIPS
(*WITH THAT "SPECIAL SOMEBODY"*), PART 2

We don't have any evidence to back this up, but we believe the average length of a romantic relationship in middle school is about three weeks. That means some people stay together for a few months and others stay together for only a few days—or a few hours. Kurt may hold the record for the world's shortest romance. In eighth grade he asked a girl to "go around" at the beginning of health class, and she broke up with him before the class was over! Ouch.

Something very strange happens as soon as you and that "special somebody" decide to become more than just friends. When you decide to start "dating," "going together," "seeing each other," or whatever you want to call it, you've crossed a line—a line that can never be uncrossed. You've officially declared that you like each other...really *like* each other!

Before you started dating each other, everything seemed so natural and easy. You didn't care about what you wore when you were around each other. You could snort like a pig when you laughed, and it was no big deal. The two of you were just friends, and friends snort like pigs in front of each other all the time. But by becoming boyfriend and girlfriend, you've now crossed an important emotional line. Things between the two of you will probably never be the same.

All the stuff we talked about in the last chapter hurts your relationship with your friends, but it also hurts the relationship you're trying to have with your new boyfriend or girlfriend. And, as if that's not enough, things get really crazy when you break up because anytime a relationship ends, feelings get hurt, people get angry, people get embarrassed, and things get confusing. All this stuff can end up ruining what used to be a really good friendship with somebody of the opposite sex. And, unfortunately, things between the two of you will probably never be as good as they were before you started dating.

By the way, you WILL break up. The odds of you marrying your middle school sweetheart are about a million to one. Or, as Marko's dad used to say, "The odds are slim to none, and slim just left town."

So before you move on from being "just friends," you and your soon-to-be "special somebody" might ask yourselves this question: *Is a three-week relationship really worth sacrificing our friendships with our other buddies and with each other?*

PHYSICAL STUFF
(HOW FAR IS TOO FAR?)

It's highly likely this is the first chapter you've read in this book. Maybe you looked at the Table of Contents, saw the title of this chapter, and said to yourself, *Forget about all that other junk. I'm going right to the good stuff!*

When we talk to middle schoolers about sex and dating, the most popular question we get asked is, *How far is too far?* The curiosity surrounding the answer to that question is why some of our readers will skip right to this chapter. After all, most of you already know God wants you to wait until you're married to have sex, but how far can you go in the meantime?

"Going too far" in God's eyes is probably not as far as you think. Most Christian teenagers want to draw some sort of magical line and then try not to cross it. And the majority of them will assume the forbidden line is sexual intercourse. We've discovered that more and more Christian teenagers are going way too far these days, but they believe it's still okay because they haven't "gone all the way."

What we think: We believe the question of *How far is too far?* is actually the wrong question to ask. The right question is more like, *How should I treat this person in a way that respects her?* or, *What type of behavior would God approve of?* Wanting to know just how far you can physically go with somebody doesn't really get to the heart of the issue, which is this: When it comes to sexual behavior, you need to develop a desire to please God and to respect the person you're dating. And these desires need to be a lot bigger than your desire to see how far you can go without getting your hand slapped.

What we know: We know the worst place to get advice when it comes to sexual behavior is places like MTV, the movies, and *Seventeen* magazine. Talk to your parents and your youth pastor to hear what they think. You could even read the Bible to learn more about some of God's thoughts on sex. After all, God created it.

HOW TO BREAK UP WELL

Okay, what do you do once you decide it's time to end a relationship with your "special somebody"? Remember, since most middle school romances last only a few weeks, if you have a boyfriend or girlfriend now, then the odds are pretty good that a breakup is in your near future.

In this chapter we're going to give you a few thoughts about how to break up with someone in a healthy way. Then in the next chapter, we'll take a look at how to handle it when someone breaks up with you.

How to break up well:

Pray about it. God wants to be involved in every part of your life. Ask God to help you break up well.

Talk to the person face-to-face. Look, if you're old enough to have a boyfriend or girlfriend, then you're old enough to put an end to the relationship face-to-face. Don't have a friend tell him, don't pass him a note in science class, and don't send him an IM.

Be honest. Don't try to make it easier on him (or easier on yourself) by coming up with some lame excuse. Be honest about the reasons why you're putting an end to the relationship. If he has bad breath—tell him. If she treats you poorly and is overly jealous—tell her. If you've decided you just don't like him in that special way anymore—tell him.

"I just want to be friends" is actually a pretty good line. Hopefully you and your boyfriend or girlfriend will be able to figure out how to keep being friends after the romantic part of the relationship has come to an end. If you use this line as part of your breakup strategy, make sure you mean it and you're willing to work to keep the friendship alive.

Be ready for things to get wacky. There's a pretty good chance the person you're breaking up with will be hurt, frustrated, and maybe even angry. He may cry. She may punch you or spread a nasty rumor about you. When this stuff happens, ask God to help you respond in a way that honors him.

Breaking up is hard to do. Doing it well is even harder. But breaking up well is always the right thing to do.

GETTING DUMPED

STUFF YOU CAN TEACH YOUR FRIENDS: AT ANY ONE TIME, THERE ARE 100 MILLION PHONE CONVERSATIONS GOING ON IN THE UNITED STATES.

It's called lots of stuff: Getting broken up with, getting dropped, getting kicked to the curb, getting dumped, and so on. But no matter what it's called, it always feels lousy. When someone breaks up with you, how should you respond?

Your answer might be, "Well, that all depends on how he treats me when he dumps me. If he's nice, I'll be nice. But if he's mean, I'll be mean right back!" Even though that answer might make sense, it's probably not the best way to approach the experience. No matter how someone breaks up with you, there are two things to think about that will help you handle the situation in the best way possible.

First, don't let yourself hold a grudge against the person. It's weird how breakups work. An hour before you get dumped, you think your "special somebody" is the greatest thing since the invention of toilet paper. However, as soon as the breakup happens—we're talking, at the exact same *second* you get dumped—he becomes nothing more than the stuff toilet paper was created to clean up. When someone breaks up with you, it's natural to feel hurt and confused. Try to avoid paying the person back by saying mean things, treating him poorly, spreading rumors about him, and so on. Holding a grudge against the person who broke up with you doesn't hurt him at all. In fact, you end up hurting only yourself.

Second, don't let a breakup change how you feel about *you.* Please read this next paragraph very carefully. Your value as a young man or woman has NOTHING to do with whether or not you have a girlfriend or boyfriend. You're an amazing, awesome, custom masterpiece who was handmade by God! You're special because you're God's kid, not because you're "going with" someone. You're valuable because you were created in God's image, not because someone of the opposite sex thought you were cute. We live in a crazy society that makes romance and all that stuff seem way more important than it really is. Don't let the fact that somebody broke up with you change the truth about you—you're wonderful, awesome, amazing, and valuable! And that's true whether or not you're dating.

Getting dumped is no fun, but you'll bounce back. Marko got dumped approximately 71 times in middle school, and look how he turned out!

Ah...never mind.

WHAT KIND OF DATING MAKES THE MOST SENSE?

By now you may be wondering if we have anything *good* to say about this whole of idea of becoming more than friends while you're in middle school. On the one hand, we're saying it's totally natural. But on the other hand, we're also saying there's a whole bunch of junk that can happen, like going too far, hurting someone's feelings, dealing with jealousy, and surviving the unavoidable breakups. Is there a good way to date in middle school? Is there a way to experience some of the stuff that's natural at your age without experiencing all of the junk that usually comes along with it? Yes. Maybe. Kinda. Sorta.

Warning: If you decide to start dating in middle school, you're getting involved in something that's really hard to do well. Lots and lots of people who are older and wiser than you still haven't figured out this whole dating thing yet. But if you insist on having a boyfriend or a girlfriend, at least let us share some of our thoughts about it.

Thought #1: There's safety in numbers. What we mean is that the best way to date during the teenage years is to "group date." A group date is when, instead of being out on a date alone, you and your "special somebody" go out with a group of friends. Group dating is safer than a solo date for lots of reasons, but one of the biggest is that group dating keeps things from getting too serious too quickly.

Thought #2: Avoid the terms *boyfriend* and *girl-friend*. Saying things like "We really like each other," "We like doing stuff together," or "We're more than just friends" are good ways to express how you feel about each other without the seriousness of calling each other "boyfriend and girlfriend."

Thought #3: Never start dating unless your parents say it's okay. In other words, don't go out with someone behind your parents' backs. Never do this. Never, *ever* do this. Seriously, don't do this! Dating is serious stuff, and you need to talk about it with your parents first.

Thought #4: Maybe the kind of dating that makes the most sense is not dating at all. We'll talk about this in the next chapter.

IT'S OKAY TO WAIT TO DATE

We've spent the last seven chapters talking about the opposite sex and dating. We did this because we know it's a huge deal for many of you reading this book. Before we move on to other stuff, we want to wrap up this section by saying this: IT'S OKAY TO WAIT TO DATE. In fact, we'll take that a step further: IT'S *BETTER* TO WAIT TO DATE.

We know you probably feel the pressure to start dating in middle school, and maybe it seems like everybody else is happily playing the dating game. So why shouldn't you?

We've talked to hundreds of grown-ups who waited to start dating until they were a little older, and guess what? None of them regretted waiting. It's true; not one of them has ever told us they wish they'd started dating earlier. We've also talked to lots and lots of adults who started dating when they were in their early teens, and guess what? Most of them wish they'd waited until they were a little older and more prepared to handle all the pressures and stuff that goes along with dating.

Here are a few interesting facts:

- The younger you are when you start dating, the more likely you are to have sex before you're married.

- The younger you are when you start dating, the more likely you are to become pregnant or to get somebody pregnant before you're married.

- The younger you are when you start dating, the more likely you are to get divorced some day.

We aren't sharing that stuff to scare you (okay, maybe we are just a little bit) but because it's true. That doesn't mean these things will automatically happen to you if you start dating while you're in middle school. It just means they're *more likely* to happen.

Middle school is a crazy, confusing, and sometimes scary time of your life. Why make it even crazier, more confusing, and scarier by adding a boyfriend or girlfriend to the mix? You have enough things to worry about.

When it's done right, dating is a really cool part of growing up. We think it's also something worth waiting for!

WHY DOES CONFLICT EXIST IN FRIENDSHIPS?

It happens like this: You and your good friend have been friends for a while, and you've never really had a fight. Until last week. Your friend did something that really, really hurt you, but when you tried to talk about it, your friend just blew you off and then ignored you. And that just added to the hurt. Now you're not sure how you can ever be friends anymore.

Or maybe it happens like this: You and your friend seem to fight all the time. Sometimes it's over little things that seem so stupid you can hardly believe you fought about it. And sometimes it's over bigger things. The two of you usually patch things up, but there's probably going to be another argument very soon.

Or maybe you don't really "fight" with your friend. When things aren't okay with your friend, maybe you experience coldness or a lack of communication between the two of you. You're not even sure what happened or if there was something specific that brought on the problems. They're just there.

There are lots of reasons for conflict (which includes fighting, disagreements, tension, misunderstandings, arguments) in friendships, but we're going to name two that are the most common to middle school students:

First, conflict is normal in all relationships. That's because we're ALL messed-up, imperfect people. *Everyone* sins (Romans 3:23 says, "For all have sinned..."). And when we sin, it often has a hurtful impact on someone else. That's not an excuse to hurt your friends and then say, "Well, I'm a sinner just like you, so it's normal that I hurt you."

Second, conflict is even more normal in middle school friendships because of all the change that's going on in your life right now. Seriously, you're like a change-a-zoid, a change-master, a transformer. You're shifting from one you (a kid) to a new you (a young adult). And it's a messy change full of bumps and surprises and sharp corners and questions and hurts. So when you and your friend are *both* changing at the rate and magnitude you are, it should be no surprise that there will be conflict from time to time.

> "I HATE IT WHEN MY FRIENDS ACT LIKE IT'S NO BIG DEAL WHEN THEY DO SOMETHING THAT BOTHERS ME OR HURTS MY FEELINGS."
>
> —KENDALL, 7TH GRADE

JEALOUSY

You've got a pretty cool gaming system, but your friend has a newer, sweeter one. And you want it so bad!

Your friend has the coolest dad. He's fun and hip and seems to be really caring. And *your* dad? Well, he left when you were a kid. Sometimes you feel something almost like anger that you don't have a dad like your friend's.

You studied your pickin' brains out for the history test, and you were sure you knew everything. But you still got a B-, while your friend who didn't study *at all* got an A. ARGH! It's so frustrating! You wanted that A, and your friend does *not* deserve it!

Your friend's family went to Europe for a family vacation this year. You could hardly believe it. The only vacation you took was a weekend spent at Grandma's house where there's nothing to do and it's boring, boring, boring. And the whole time you were there, you dreamt about what it would be like to vacation in Europe.

None of these little stories might be an exact fit for you, but we think you get the idea. Change a few details, and we all have little stories like this in our lives. It's called *jealousy*. (Yeah, it's spelled weird, but you know the word—JELL-us-see.)

Jealousy is when you wish you had what someone else has. You can be jealous of a thing, like your friend's gaming system. Or you can be jealous of a characteristic, like your friend getting an A on the test when your friend didn't even study (because, obviously, your friend is either really smart or really good at taking tests). Or you can be jealous of a situation, like your friend's family going to Europe on vacation.

Jealousy can have a big, bad impact on friendships. It's not the kind of thing that usually leads to a fight, but it slowly eats away at a friendship because friendships thrive on the things you have in common, and jealousy points out how different you are.

So when you find yourself feeling jealous toward your friend (for whatever reason), try to name the jealousy to yourself and then throw it away. Ask God to help you get rid of your jealousy and be happy with who you are and what you have.

SELFISHNESS

"It's mine, mine, mine! And you can't have it!"

Have you ever heard a little kid say something like that? It's usually accompanied by stamping feet and tight fists and a shrieking, high-pitched voice. Doesn't exactly make you want to hug the kid, does it?

Well, that kind of behavior doesn't end when you grow up. In fact, adults do it all the time—it just looks different (most of the time). Adults are sneakier about their selfishness, but they (we) can still be totally and massively selfish.

And guess what? Surprise, surprise (no surprise at all, really)—so can you. *Selfishness* is thinking only of yourself. So if you're selfish about *stuff*, it looks like you're hoarding all the *stuff* for yourself. If you're selfish about *opportunities*, it looks like you're putting yourself first. If you're selfish about *attention*, it looks like you're making sure everyone else notices you.

Selfishness is the opposite of everything Jesus talks about. A selfish person says, "I want all the stuff." Jesus says to give your stuff away (Matthew 19:21). A selfish person says, "I want all the opportunities." Jesus says to put others first (Matthew 22:39). A selfish person says, "Notice me!" And Jesus says, "The last will be first, and the first will be last" (Matthew 20:16).

So it makes sense that if selfishness is the opposite of what Jesus wants for us, and if Jesus is the inventor of friendship, then selfishness is harmful to friendships. Really, it's kind of obvious, isn't it? Good friendships are built on giving and caring and respect.

Think of it this way: Selfish people never have friends for long.

Or put it this way: Selfishness kills friendships.

Or how about this way: If you want to have great friendships, stop being selfish!

GOSSIP (PROVERBS 16:28)

"Psst. Know what? Ohmygoshyouhavetohearthisit's-sojuicy. Justin told me that Kendra told him that Carly heard that Josh has a massive crush on Suzy!"

"That's not what I heard. I heard Cassie is actually a guy!"

"No way! And you know what else? Someone said Emily is...ohmygosh, this is so amazing...Emily is actually a space alien!"

Okay. Maybe the gossip you hear and repeat doesn't get that weird. But it might as well be that weird sometimes. Whether or not it's true isn't even the point.

Gossip (talking about people behind their backs, sharing information about people that doesn't have any benefit because it's all just juicy stories to tell) hurts people. God is clearly against it, and it can destroy friendships.

Check out Proverbs 16:28:

"A GOSSIP SEPARATES CLOSE FRIENDS."

That says it pretty bluntly, huh?

This might be the opposite of what you've experienced. You might be thinking, "But it seems like gossip can actually *help* a friendship. Like, me and my friend gossip, and it's part of what we love to do together."

Here's the problem. Gossip might *seem* fun in a friendship for a while, but eventually you'll realize that if your friend gossips *to* you all the time, then she's probably willing to gossip *about* you to others. That's the way it works: People who gossip all the time don't know how to turn it on and off. They just gossip all the time.

So sooner or later gossip becomes a friendship killer because it destroys the trust in a friendship.

Sure, God can't stand gossip, even if you feel like it's adding some fun to your friendship. And sure, gossip always ends up hurting people, which God can't stand, either. But ultimately, gossip is a friendship killer.

INSECURITY

You might not know what *insecurity* means. So we'll take a crack at explaining it before we talk about why it can hurt friendships.

When something is *secure*, that means it won't move or change; it means it's safe. Like, when a bolt on the side of a ship is secure, that means the bolt isn't going to come loose and fall off. And when that same ship is secure in a harbor, it's in a place where nothing can harm it (weather, enemies, and so on).

Of course, the opposite would also be true: When something is *insecure*, it's *not* safe, and it could change at any moment.

People can also be secure or insecure. In fact, we're all usually one or the other. Someone who's secure is sure of herself; she's confident. She feels safe (whether or not she really is). Someone who is *insecure*, then, is the opposite of that: She is *not* comfortable with who she is, she is *not* confident, and she does *not* feel safe.

Just because someone is outgoing and social, that doesn't mean she's secure. In fact, lots of people who seem really social and outgoing act that way *because* they're insecure and want people to like them.

Stop for a minute and think. Are you secure or insecure?

Here's what this has to do with friendship. A friendship between two secure people can have a different kind of strength than a friendship where one or both of the friends are insecure. Insecurity causes people not to be themselves. It drives people to be needy, to act the way they think others want them to act, and to constantly look for hidden meanings behind what others say and do.

Bottom line—insecurity hurts a friendship because it doesn't allow you to really be yourself. And friendships thrive when there's honesty and when people can be totally real with each other.

On the other hand, insecurity can lead to conflict in a friendship, since one or both friends aren't being totally honest. Insecurity demands more from a friendship than is fair to expect, and it also expects levels of commitment that aren't always realistic or fair.

FORGIVENESS

Fact—You'll hurt your friends.

Fact—Your friends will hurt you.

That doesn't make it right or easy. It just is. We're humans, and we sin, and we'll always end up hurting others (and ourselves).

So when you have conflict with a friend—either because one of you hurt the other one, or because you just disagree on something—forgiveness becomes a HUGE part of friendship survival.

I (Marko) remember a time during middle school when I was performing in a skit with a couple of my friends at a youth group retreat. We were carrying one of the guys, who happened to be one of my best friends, on a board. (He was supposed to be an alien king or something stupid like that.) And then in the middle of the skit, I thought it would be really funny to let go of the board and drop him. I have no idea *why* I thought this would be funny; but I did it anyway.

It wasn't funny.

He dropped like a rock and landed wrong on his arm, breaking it. My buddy had to go to the hospital, where the doctor set the bone and put a cast on his arm. When he asked me why I dropped him, all I could say was, "I thought it would be funny."

He and I are still friends today (more than 30 years later), but *only* because he chose to forgive me for my complete and total stupidity. It would have been understandable if he'd said, "Marko, you are just too big of an idiot—a complete loser, really—and I cannot be your friend anymore." But he forgave me so we could continue our friendship.

I broke his other arm later that same year, but that's another story. (See the "I Was a Middle School Dork" story on page 152.)

You *will* have conflicts with your friends. So if you want to keep friends, you'll have to be willing to forgive them. The apostle Paul said, "Bear with each other and forgive whatever grievances you may have against one another. Forgive as the Lord forgave you" (Colossians 3:13).

> "I QUIT BEING FRIENDS WITH SOMEBODY OVER SOMETHING DUMB. NOW I'M WORKING HARD TO BE FRIENDS AGAIN."
> —ZACK, 6TH GRADE

PEER PRESSURE

We're sure you've heard of *peer pressure*, even though we know it's really an adult phrase and no normal middle schooler would talk about *peer pressure*. Or at least they wouldn't use those words. "Peers" is just another way of saying "friends" or "people you hang out with." So peer pressure is just a fancy way of talking about when your friends—or others your own age—pressure you to do things.

Peer pressure can be good. Like, if your friends encourage you to do good things, then that's still considered peer pressure, but it's a good thing. But more often, peer pressure is the reason we make lousy choices. We want our friends to like us and think we're cool. And if they're choosing to do something (even if it's something we don't really want to do or don't think we should do), then we feel like we need to go along with them or they might think we're total losers.

Why did we put the "Peer Pressure" chapter in the "Conflict" section of this book? Because peer pressure can often lead to conflict in friendships. Here's an example:

When I (Marko) was in middle school, one of my buddies started playing around with cigarettes. I say "playing around" because he didn't smoke regularly at all—he just thought it was cool, and he smoked once in a while. I was there one time when he and some of his other friends were smoking. They asked me if I wanted to smoke, and I said I didn't. They started teasing me and telling me I was a wuss. So I smoked a cigarette to get them off my back.

This situation caused a conflict between my friend and me that lasted for a year. I didn't want to hang around him anymore because he'd pressured me into doing something I didn't want to do.

It's a lot harder for people you don't really know to pressure you into doing things you don't want to do or you know you shouldn't do. But when *friends* pressure you—well, it's harder to say "no." You'll often end up questioning the friendship because it felt like your friend didn't really care about your opinion.

A few quick thoughts:

1. Like we've said so many times in this book already: This is normal. It's a struggle *not* to pressure your friends to do things you want to do. You'll deal with this your whole life.

2. If you feel as if a friend is pressuring you to do something you don't want to do, it's important you tell him so.

3. When peer pressure brings conflict into your friendship, there's no way to get past it other than to talk about it. Be honest about how your friend made you feel, but also be quick to forgive your friend.

"PEER PRESSURE—IT'S A GIANT, BUT FIGHT IT LIKE DAVID DID AND KILL IT!"
—GRANT, 8TH GRADE

HOW TO RESOLVE CONFLICT

By now (if you've read the other little chapters in this section), you've seen that conflict is a normal part of all relationships and certainly all friendships. We could write entire books about how to deal with conflict in friendships. (In fact, lots of books *have* been written on this subject.) But we'll stick with a few basics here:

First, if you're the cause of conflict in your friendship (and you will be just as often as you won't be), own it. Be honest with yourself, with God, and with your friend. Ask for forgiveness from your friend, and try to think about how you can avoid repeating your actions that brought on the conflict.

Second, anytime there's conflict in a friend-ship, you have to talk about it. This is a lot easier for girls to do than it is for guys. Girls are much better at talking about their feelings. But talking about it is massively important. And don't be mean about it when you talk. Don't say, "You're a to-tal jerk, and I need to make sure you know that!" That's not *talking about it*, that's name-calling.

Third, get help if the conflict is serious. You can always walk away from the friendship, but it's way better to save the friendship if you can. And sometimes, when the conflict seems huge and dif-ficult, it's really helpful to have a third person in-volved, maybe even an...adult. (Sorry, we had to say it.) The third person needs to be someone who's neutral (that means she won't just side with one person for personal reasons). That's why an adult can often be helpful.

Fourth, pray about it. God created friendship, and God wants you to have wonderful and fun and meaningful friendships. So when you have conflict in your friendship, God would love to be part of the solution. Ask God for wisdom and ideas. Ask God to help you save the friendship and not be mean to your friend in the process.

Finally, know this: Sometimes (not all the time) conflict in a friendship is a good sign that you need to find different friends. Seriously, if you're constantly having conflict with your friend or friends, you might want to consider whether or not they're the right friends for you. You just might find you're trying to make the friendship work for all the wrong reasons (because they were popular or something like that).

"ME AND MY FRIENDS SEEM TO ARGUE A LOT, BUT WE GET OVER IT PRETTY QUICK."

—SKYLER, 8TH GRADE

I WAS A MIDDLE SCHOOL DORK! —KURT

In eighth grade, I played football for the La Mirada Bears. No one—not my wife, my own children, or the kids in my youth group—will believe this, but I was pretty good. Our team made it to the championship, and along the way I set a league record for most catches and was named to the All-Star team. I was a tough guy, a man's man, a dude's dude, Mr. Macho—at least I thought I was. But that all changed after the championship game.

We were facing the Steelers, a team we'd played twice that season. In our first two meetings, we'd beaten them once, and they'd beaten us once. We entered the championship with the exact same season records. The crowd was huge. Parents, friends, relatives, and just about every player from the other teams in the league gathered along the sidelines to watch the match-up.

I played a pretty good game. I intercepted one pass and caught another one for a touchdown. We played well and so did the Steelers. It was one for the ages. We were tied with about two minutes to go, when the Steelers intercepted a pass and ran it all the way back for a touchdown. When the gun sounded at the end of the game, the scoreboard showed everybody what I'd hoped wouldn't happen: Steelers 21, Bears 14.

I was sad—really sad! As we shook hands with the Steelers after the game, I could feel the tears trying to fight their way out of my eyeballs, but I wasn't about to let that happen because I was a tough guy, a man's man, a dude's dude, Mr. Macho—at least I thought I was.

Everybody gathered at the 50-yard line for the trophy ceremony: championship trophies for the Steelers and second-place trophies for us Bears. As I stood there, my mom suddenly appeared out of nowhere. She walked right up to me, gave me a massive hug, and kissed me right on the cheek. At that moment I totally melted. I lost all control and began crying right there in front of everybody. I'm not talking about a little, sissy cry. I'm talking about a big, loud, snot-filled, body-shaking, wail-your-head-off kind of cry. The kind that everybody notices. My coaches noticed, my teammates noticed, and, worst of all, the Steelers noticed.

So what did this tough guy, man's man, dude's dude, Mr. Macho do? I suddenly realized what I was doing, and I sprinted to the car as fast as I could. And what did my mom and dad do? They stuck around to watch the rest of the trophy ceremony.

WAYS TO BE A GOOD FRIEND

LOYALTY

When a captive soldier doesn't give away military secrets—even when he's threatened with his life—he's considered loyal.

When a customer eats burgers only from McHappy's and won't eat burgers from any other burger place, she's considered loyal.

When a dog goes to great lengths to find her way home after being lost, she's considered loyal.

When a married couple sticks together for years and years and years and neither one of them ever messes around with anyone else, they're considered loyal.

God is loyal to us—always committed to us, never changing or letting us down. Jesus proved his loyalty to us by dying on the cross. That's big-time loyalty.

And that quality of loyalty—which you could also call "faithfulness"—is a HUGE way in which you can be a good friend.

When I (Marko) was a teenager, I made a really bad choice that caused a lot of people to be angry with me. But I remember one friend who came to me and said, "I might not like what you did, but I'm your friend and I'm sticking with you." That kind of loyalty in a friendship is so cool, so wonderful, and so hard to find.

How can you be loyal to your friends? Try being committed to them no matter what. That doesn't mean you always have to agree with them. But it does mean your friendship isn't based on surface things like whether or not they're always fun, or whether or not they're always nice to you. A loyal friend doesn't say one thing, and then do another. A loyal friend doesn't tell secrets. A loyal friend doesn't bolt at the first hint of conflict, but is committed to working through the tough stuff.

Friendships that last a long time—like, for years and years—are built on a rock-solid foundation of loyalty. We hope you can find that kind of friend. We hope you can be that kind of friend.

HONESTY

STUFF YOU CAN TEACH YOUR FRIENDS: THE CITRUS-FLAVORED SODA CALLED "7UP" WAS CREATED IN 1929. THE "7" WAS SELECTED BECAUSE THE ORIGINAL CONTAINERS HELD SEVEN OUNCES, AND "UP" INDICATED THE DIRECTION OF THE BUBBLES.

We're all looking for a friend we can trust. Nothing hurts more than when someone lies to you, especially when that someone is a friend. A good friend is honest.

What is honesty? Honesty is simply communicating the truth. You say what you mean. Honesty doesn't mean you don't care about someone's feelings or you say things that are mean just because they're true. Honesty in a friendship means to speak the truth in a loving, straightforward way.

Let's say Marko came up to me (Kurt) in front of a group of people and said, "Kurt, you're short, you're balding, your feet are small, that shirt is so 1997, and you have hair coming out of your ears." Is he being honest? Unfortunately, YES. Is there a better place and time for him to tell me these things? Definitely. Or maybe he doesn't have to say them at all because they're obvious, unnecessary, and won't build me up. If you don't say something that's true because you feel it's not going to help the situation or the person, then it's not dishonesty. That's showing good judgment.

Being honest doesn't involve gossiping about your friends to other people. When you talk behind a friend's back—even if everything you say is the truth—it's not encouraging them or building them up. Again, when honesty is used in the wrong way, it can be disastrous to a friendship.

Sometimes the truth hurts. If you're going to be honest with your friends, then you have to be prepared for them to be honest with you. Don't expect to just dish it out without them dishing it right back at you. If a friend says something to you that hurts, be honest with her. Tell her it hurt, and also explain *why* it hurt. This kind of honest sharing will only strengthen your friendship and build trust between you.

Honesty is always the best policy. A friendship built around complete honesty will be solid. A friendship built around honesty plus good judgment will produce a friendship that lasts a lifetime.

> "I THINK THE MOST IMPORTANT QUALITY IN A FRIEND IS HONESTY. THAT AND SOMEBODY WHO ISN'T EMBARRASSED WHEN THEY FART OUT LOUD."
>
> —MATTHEW, 8TH GRADE

ENCOURAGEMENT

The other day, one of my (Marko's) friends said to me, "You're really good at blah, blah, blah." (Well, my friend actually told me what he thought I was good at. He didn't just say "blah, blah, blah.") It was SO encouraging.

Another friend sent me an e-mail just to tell me he enjoys how I do something-or-other. And it was SO encouraging.

We'll let you in on a little friendship secret here: If you're a person who encourages people, everyone will want to be your friend because you make people feel good about themselves.

The word *encourage* is such a cool word, once you understand it. It means "to have a full heart" or "to fill the heart." The middle syllable—*cour*—is a variation of the French word for *heart*.

And that's what it feels like when someone encourages you, doesn't it? It feels like they're filling up your heart, giving you hope and courage and strength, and making you feel strong and secure. Man, that's such a great feeling!

But there's a difference between really great encouragement and just so-so encouragement. The so-so encouragement is more surface stuff (let's call them compliments). Like, if someone tells you, "Oh, I like your hair." Well, that's nice to hear and all, and you're probably happy to have someone tell you that. But it doesn't really sustain you. It's like eating a piece of candy, rather than a home-cooked meal.

The really great encouragement is when you can point out something deeper about a person, like one of her good qualities. For instance, if you tell a friend, "You're a really creative person" (assuming she actually *is* creative), that's so much better than saying, "I like your shirt." Or you might notice your friend doing something amazing and point it out. Like, "I thought it was so cool how you were friendly to that girl in gym class, the one no one else would talk to." Yup—so much better than, "Your teeth are sparkly."

So try to notice the deeper things about your friends—their character and the good things they do. Then name those things and point them out. That's such a great way to be a good friend. Seriously. No, really. We're *not* kidding!

GIVING AND SERVING

In section 6 of this book (the one about conflicts in friendships), we talked about selfishness (see chapter 38) and how it can kill a good friendship. So it makes sense that the opposite of selfishness would help build up a friendship, right?

Well, the opposite of selfishness is giving and serving your friend. We're not talking about you putting on a servant's uniform and waiting on your friend. ("Yes, sir, may I get you another cup of tea?") No, we're talking about trying to meet your friend's deeper needs.

The problem is most middle schoolers don't take their eyes off themselves long enough to notice anyone else's needs. And that's understandable, since you're going through such a major change in your life. (It's only natural to be a bit self-focused right now, even if it's not a great thing.)

What kinds of needs might your friend have that you could meet? Well, many of them are probably the same as yours. Like, you probably have a need to feel valued or to feel like you're special. So it's probably true that your friend has that same need, and you can probably do something to meet that need. Or maybe you realize you need someone you can share your deepest secrets with. So it would make sense that your friend probably has the same need.

There might also be some things your friend needs that you *don't* need. For instance, you might notice how your friend can't afford to buy a new pair of jeans, and she always wears the same pair that are really kind of worn out. Maybe you can meet that need. Or you might notice that your friend could really use some help in doing a major chore he has to do (like, raking leaves or something like that). You can serve your friend by helping him with that chore.

Or how about this one: You might be aware that your friend doesn't know Jesus. Well, that's a pretty huge need, whether or not your friend realizes it. One of the best ways you could ever, *ever* serve your friend is by telling her about Jesus and the difference Jesus has made in your life.

If you're able to learn the skill of noticing other peoples' needs and being willing to do what you can to meet them, you'll be such a better friend than most people in the world. You'll be a super-friend!

"ME AND MY BEST FRIEND WEAR THE SAME SIZE, SO WE SHARE EACH OTHER'S OUTFITS."
—KRISTY, 7TH GRADE

COMPASSION

Compassion is kind of a big word, isn't it? Do you know what it means? It has to do with feeling what other people are feeling. But it's more like being moved (emotionally) when someone else is hurting or in need and wanting to help that person.

The second half of the word says it all: *passion*. *Passion* means to be completely and totally sold out to something. Like, you can be passionate about soccer if you think about and play soccer all the time. Or you can be passionate about video games, if that's, like, the major thing in your life. Of course, you can also be passionate about another person, too.

And *com-passion* means "with passion."

So why would compassion help a friendship?

We all have hurts in our lives. We all have times when things are not going well. Sure, it's great to have someone who can actually *help* you with your problems (like, help you solve them). But sometimes we don't really need help solving them; or maybe there's nothing to be solved. Sometimes we just need someone who knows about our pain and feels for us.

That's an important trait of a good friend—someone who notices your pain and feels it, too.

As I (Marko) write this, I just got some news through an e-mail that a friend of mine is in the hospital struggling with a disease he didn't know he had. He almost died, and he easily could have lost an arm or a leg because of it. The doctors say they caught it in time, so he's probably going to be okay. But he's still going to have to spend two weeks in the hospital, and then another two months at home. Some of his other friends and I have started talking about how we can let him know we care—that we understand the pain he's in. We're thinking of gifts and visits and e-mails and prayers and all kinds of things that will communicate our love for him.

That's compassion. Do you have that for your friends?

LISTENING

I (Kurt) am not a very good listener. I'm good at sitting with someone, looking them in the face as they talk to me, but not remembering a word they say. Seriously, it's crazy! There are times when my wife will sit next to me on the couch and share her day with me. I'll look at her every few seconds, nod, and grunt, but then later I don't remember a thing she said because my mind was thinking about my own problems at work or the great football game on TV.

Everyone wants and needs someone to talk to. But more importantly, everyone needs someone who will listen. The Bible talks about the importance of listening. It says there's "a time to be silent and a time to speak" (Ecclesiastes 3:7).

Hey, girls—talking is a good thing, but listening is just as important. Believe it or not, there are times to just sit (or stand) and listen.

Guys—when you're not talking, try listening. Don't be the guy who neither talks nor listens, but just stares off into la-la land.

I recently did a survey in my middle school ministry. I asked this question: "What's the number one quality you look for in a friend?" What do you think was the most popular answer? That's right, someone who will listen. Fifty percent of the guys and a whopping 80 percent of the girls wrote this on their surveys. If this is true of our middle schoolers, I'm sure it's probably true for you, too.

We all need people who will listen to us. There are times when you just need someone who will listen to you share about your frustrations, your temptations, your battles, and your victories. The Bible says, "Everyone should be quick to listen, slow to speak" (James 1:19). So listen first, and speak second.

A man's best friend is his dog. Why? Because the dog will lie there for hours and hours as you talk its floppy ears off. And the amazing thing is, it won't say a single word back to you. All that time spent listening and no talking. We can learn a lot from our four-legged friends.

So if dogs can teach us how to listen, then they must be really smart, right? (Not really—they can't even clean up their own poop!)

"I TRY TO LISTEN TO MY FRIENDS. IT SEEMS LIKE LISTENING SHOWS THEM I CARE."
—SAMANTHA, 7TH GRADE

ATTENTIVENESS

Before we dig into this chapter, let's take a quick look at what *attentiveness* actually means. Well, after looking up the word, I (Kurt) found it means "to give special treatment or attention; thoughtfulness and consideration."

After reading the definition, my mind immediately went to Katie, a friend of mine. Katie really understands the word *attentiveness*. She knows how to give special treatment to her friends, and she's super-thoughtful. A couple of months ago I was having a really tough day—one of those days when everything goes wrong. (I seem to have a lot of those days.) I couldn't find my car keys, I was late for work, I spilled my decaf Chai tea latte on my new jeans, and so on. I finally made it to work, settled into my office, and opened my e-mail. The top e-mail in my inbox was from Katie. It was a short e-mail that simply said, *I heard you had a tough morning. I just want you to know if you need anything, I'm here.* Then a couple of minutes later, Katie walked into my office with an unspilled, decaf, Chai tea latte in her hand. It was amazing!

The cool thing is that Katie does these kinds of special things for all her friends. She's the queen of thoughtfulness and attentiveness. Let's take a look at a few ways you can show some thoughtfulness toward your friends, too.

Do the little things. An attentive person does the little things in a friendship. There's nothing too small for a good friend. Don't ever think, *Someone* *else will take care of it.* What are some little things you can do? Drop a note of encouragement in her locker. Offer to buy the next time you two go to lunch. Show up at her soccer game (and actually watch). Ask her how she did on the history test. Bring him a box of popsicles after he gets his tonsils out. These are all little things that make a big difference to your friends.

Remember the big things. There are tons of little things, but there are also a lot of big things happening in your friends' lives. What are some of these big things? Remember your friends' birthdays. Remember them on holidays (Christmas, Valentine's Day, Flag Day). Remember their special awards, drama and band performances, surgeries, the tough things they're going through, and so on. Don't let the big things pass by without doing something special or at least saying something to show you care.

Go the extra mile. Go above and beyond for your friends. They're your friends, and they deserve a little extra time, money, and effort. Don't come up short!

When you start being attentive to your friends, you'll be shocked at how attentive they become toward you.

STUFF YOU CAN TEACH YOUR FRIENDS: DIET COKE WAS INVENTED IN 1982. ORIGINALLY CALLED "DIET COCA-COLA," IT WAS THE FIRST NEW BRAND TO USE THE COCA-COLA TRADEMARK SINCE 1886.

FUN!

Wow! To read the list of things we've talked about so far, you might believe that being a good friend is super-serious. But fun is an important part of being a good friend, too.

You pretty much already know this, right? I mean, we don't have to tell you it's great to have fun with your friends. Good friends love to laugh, play, tease, joke, and goof around together. In fact, some of our favorite memories with our friends are the times when we had the most fun.

So how can you be a friend who brings the fun?

First of all, don't be offended by stuff all the time. If your friend makes a joke that kind of feels like it's teasing you, but you can tell your friend didn't mean for it to hurt you, then don't make a big deal out of it. Be willing to laugh at yourself.

Be creative. Suggest fun and new ideas for things you and your friends can do together. Make up games. Go on a hike. Rent a movie and bake cookies. Create a silly play. There are so many things you can do that will be fun, but it usually requires someone suggesting it in the first place.

Be spontaneous. That means do stuff now—without thinking about it too much. The most fun you'll ever have with your friends probably won't be the times you plan ahead. Instead, they'll be the crazy ideas that strike you, and then you take off and do something nutty.

Be careful how you tease. It seems fun, sometimes, to tease your friends. Especially when they do stupid things. But teasing them can be hurtful, too, and it can cause them not to feel safe with you. Tease your friends only if you know they'll think it's funny.

When I (Marko) was in middle school, my buddy and I would camp out in a tent in his backyard sometimes. It was kind of lame in some ways. I mean, we weren't at a campground, and we still went in the house all the time to get stuff we needed or wanted. But to us, it was so much fun: playing flashlight wars, telling scary stories, eating junk food, and all that stuff. Those fun times strengthened our friendship.

Do you add fun to your friendships?

FLEXIBILITY

Do you know what *flexibility* is? It's when something is bendy. Like, a garden hose is flexible. And a piece of paper is flexible. But a rock isn't flexible. And a metal pipe isn't flexible.

People can either be flexible or inflexible (*not* flexible). And that's not referring to whether or not they can bend in half. (Well, actually, it can also mean that. After all, a gymnast who can contort her body into weird shapes is considered flexible. But that's not the kind of flexibility we're talking about here.)

No, the kind of flexible we're talking about is when people are willing to change. Sometimes you'd even say those people are willing to "bend."

So why is flexibility a way to be a good friend? Well, it's hard to be friends with people who are never, ever willing to change.

Let's say you and your friend go to the mall. While you're there, you decide to see a movie. Your friend wants to see a movie that you've already seen and didn't like. You want to see almost anything *but* that movie. Your friend won't budge, and she insists she won't be happy unless you agree to go to the movie you don't want to see. That's inflexibility. And it stinks up a friendship.

Really, being *flexible* means you're willing to give up your own plans and your own agenda. That communicates to your friends that you think they're important—or that what matters to them also matters to you.

Good friends are flexible friends. Be bendy!

ACCOUNTABILITY

We talked about the power of friends in chapter 8 and discovered we're stronger when we share life with others. In a Christ-centered friendship, we need to be on the lookout for each other and keep each other *accountable*. (In fact, that's what accountability means—looking out for each other.) It's like when teammates go to each other and point out flaws and mistakes in order to help each other become better players. Let's take a look at a couple of ways you can be a good accountability partner with your friends.

Be confidential. The first step to being accountable to your friends is to be careful with what they tell you. They're not going to share stuff with you if you can't keep it to yourself. After a friend spills her personal problems and struggles, keep it to yourself. This tells your friend, *You can trust me to do what's right.* Being confidential means you keep most stuff to yourself, but not everything. If a friend shares something dangerous, scary, or harmful, you need to let somebody else know. Tell her you're going to talk to a parent, school counselor, or youth pastor. If you can be trusted, you'll attract friends who are the same way. Are you reliable? Or would someone be stupid to trust you?

Be honest. Confidentiality leads to honesty. If you can keep things to yourself, your friends will be open and honest when they share with you. Accountability is honestly sharing your struggles and hurts with each other and keeping those struggles a secret. Again, people are looking for friends they can trust. How difficult is it for you to keep a secret? How difficult is it for you to share what you're really dealing with? If you're not honest with each other, there won't be any accountability.

Be respectful. If you're going to keep each other accountable, you must respect each other. When you respect a friend, you'll love and accept her for who she is, no matter what stupid decisions she makes. Respect is treating her the way you want to be treated.

The glue that holds accountability together is trust. Can you be trusted with the little and big issues in life? It might be easy for your friend to ask you to help her stop gossiping. But can she trust you enough to share how she messed up at a party she wasn't even supposed to go to? Be a friend who can be trusted. Remember, you'll find good friends by *being* a good friend.

WAYS TO BE A BAD FRIEND

COMPETING

We just gave you a pretty good list of some ways you can be a good friend. It's not a complete list, but it's a good start. There are also some ways you can be a bad friend—a bunch of attitudes and actions that, if you decide to put them into motion, will almost always mess up your friendships. Again, this list of bad behaviors isn't a complete list, either, but it's a pretty good start. Let's begin with the danger of competing with your friends.

Not all competition is bad. We're not talking about competing in a game of street football or a rousing game of UNO. That type of competition is actually a pretty healthy part of friendship. But you can mess up a friendship by being too competitive in other ways. Here are a few examples of the type of competition we're talking about.

Competing by comparing. When you constantly compare yourself to your friends, you're setting up your friendship to take a fall. Comparing is a seemingly harmless form of competition that leads to all kinds of problems. *Am I smarter than he is? Is she prettier than I am? Why isn't my house as nice as theirs?* These types of comparisons usually lead to jealousy, which, as you probably already read in chapter 37, is deadly to a friendship.

Competing for attention. When you begin competing with your friends for attention, you're beginning to chip away at your friendship. Competing for attention is just another form of selfishness. When you want all the attention, you're basically saying to your friends, *You aren't as important as I am.* When your friends feel like all you care about is yourself, they'll begin to look for a more loyal friend.

Competing for the last word. Does either of the following scenes sound familiar? You and your friend are having a disagreement. Instead of valuing her input or just letting it rest, you make sure you get the last word. Or your friend is telling a story, and you keep jumping in to make sure he tells it right. When you constantly do this kind of stuff, you're telling your friend that what you have to say is more important.

We live in a competitive world. Competition isn't always a bad thing, but it can quickly ruin friendships if we let it creep into areas of our relationships where it doesn't belong.

USING PEOPLE

You want to let this kid in your math class know you're really ticked at him, but you don't want to talk to him directly. So you ask your friend to tell the kid for you. You've just "used" your friend.

You didn't finish your science homework, but you know your friend did. You ask your friend to let you copy off his paper. When he says he's not comfortable with that, you pout and say that if he's really your friend, then he'll help you. You're using your friend.

You know your friend has more money than you do. So when you're at the store, you make a big scene about how badly you want a new CD, but how you just don't have the money to buy it. Your friend buys it for you. You've just used your friend.

"Using people" is when we treat others as a way to get what we want. Either we make people do things for us, or we convince them to, or we trick them into it. Using people shows selfishness on our part. It shows we don't really care about what's best for our friend—only about what's best for us.

Real friends—good friends—don't use each other. So if you want to be a really cruddy, lousy, terrible, stinky, awful friend, make sure you use your friends. Treat them as if they don't really matter; treat them like things, not people; treat them like they're your employees or slaves. In other words, treat them like they're *less than you are*. Yeah! Then you'll be a super-bad friend!

IGNORING

Oh, man! There may not be a better or faster way to be a bad friend than to practice the age-old art of ignoring someone. Ignoring usually takes one of two shapes. Both are bad, but you'll probably quickly discover which one does the most harm.

The first type of ignoring is when you do it by accident. This happens all the time. Your friend wants to hang out with you, but you're super-busy. So you quickly brush off your friend so you can stay focused. Or maybe you're hanging out with a group of friends. On this particular Friday night, you're giving more attention to one friend than another. You really aren't trying to be mean, and you may not even know you're ignoring your other friend. But even though you aren't doing it on purpose, her feelings still get hurt. When that happens, friendships usually get hurt, too.

You'll never get this one totally under control. (Kurt ignores Marko all the time.) However, when you notice you've been ignoring a friend, the best thing to do is quickly apologize and make a point of trying to pay better attention to your friend in the future.

The second type of ignoring is when you do it on purpose. Giving somebody the "cold shoulder," as it's called, has been a favorite practice of bad friends for thousands of years. (By the way, "cold shoulder" first appeared in the early 1800s, supposedly alluding to the custom of welcoming a desired guest with a meal of roasted meat, but serving only a cold shoulder of beef or lamb—a far inferior dish—to those who outstayed their welcomes.) Anyway, purposely ignoring somebody by giving him the silent treatment or acting as if he no longer exists is super-effective because it's so hurtful. Nobody likes to be purposely ignored by a friend.

If you try to get back at your friends by ignoring them, or if giving somebody the cold shoulder is your way of making a point or avoiding a friend, then you need to recognize you're really making it tough for that person to continue to be your friend. A friend who nervously waits for the next time you decide to ignore her probably isn't going to stay friends with you for very long.

> "FRIENDS ARE AMAZING; BUT WHEN TOUGH TIMES HIT, THEY SEEM TO RUN AWAY AND BE AFRAID TO HELP ME GRIEVE."
> —RACHEL, 8TH GRADE

BOSSINESS

"Get me this..." "Do this for me now!" "Don't do that!" "Listen to me!"

Those commands don't sound super-friendly, do they? Those commands—and a whole bunch of other ones just like 'em—are frequently used by bossy people. You want to mess up your friend-ships? Here's a tip: Start bossing your friends around.

Most people don't like to be bossed around. Grown-ups don't even like to be bossed around by their bosses, even though that's kinda what bosses are supposed to do. But since you aren't the boss of your friends (unless you're paying them to be your friends, which would be really odd), you have no reason to boss them around, and they have no reason to put up with it.

In any circle of friends, there will be one or two people who sort of rise to the top, and then everyone else views them as the leaders. This is pretty natural, but it can get bad when it results in bossiness.

If your friends happen to view you as a leader, avoid the temptation to use that position as an excuse to tell everybody how they should behave, what they should do, and when they should do it. If you're one of the leaders of the pack, your friends probably value your opinion quite a bit, so don't be afraid to share it. But try to share your opinions in a way that doesn't make your friends feel like you think you're better than they are.

If you aren't the leader of your pack, it can become really tempting to try to increase your influence by becoming bossy. You may think that by getting a little more vocal and by bossing people around, you'll improve your position within your circle of friends. There are two problems with this idea. First, that's an example of the wrong type of competition, which we talked about a few chapters ago (see chapter 54). Second, your friends will notice you've changed and you're beginning to act like a jerk. Your really good friends might be willing to pull you aside and talk to you about it, but the rest of them will just decide they don't want to be your friends anymore.

Enough about bossiness. Go ahead and read the next chapter. Read it right now! Oops...did that sound too bossy?

INSENSITIVITY

This is a big word that can do really big damage to a friendship. *Insensitivity* basically means you don't care about the other person's feelings. Because caring about each other is a basic part of friendship, it's easy to see how insensitivity is a great way to be a bad friend. Okay, that's probably pretty easy to understand. Now stick with us because it's about to get a little trickier.

Another problem with insensitivity is that the insensitive person usually has no idea they're being insensitive. It can look something like this:

> Friend #1: "I'm nervous about the test because I didn't have a chance to study."

> Friend #2: "Who cares? You stink at math anyway. It's not like studying would have helped."

Or it can look something like this:

> Friend #1: "My mom and dad seem to be fighting a lot lately, and I don't know what to do about it."

> Friend #2: "It's no big deal; my parents fight all the time. Get over it."

Or something like this:

> Marko: "Hey Kurt, what's it like to be short and bald?"

> Kurt: "It's okay. What's it like to be pudgy?"

Think about it for a second. A little joke between the two of us (like the one you just read) is kinda funny—once in a while. But if our friendship is full of insensitive moments, what kind of friendship will it be? Because so much insensitivity is done unintentionally, it's important to point it out to each other when it happens.

Good friends will thank you for pointing out their insensitivities, and they'll work on trying to be more sensitive in the future.

INSINCERITY

No, really, you're *totally* the smartest person I've ever known in my entire life!" (*Not!*)

"I would never, ever tell *anyone* your secret!" (*Except the next three people I run into!*)

"I think those jeans look great on you!" (And by "great," I mean they make your rear end look like the size of Iowa.)

When someone is *sincere*, it just means they mean what they say they mean. (We tried to figure out a way to get a fourth *mean* into that sentence, but just couldn't.) On the other hand, an insincere person says things he doesn't really mean.

Insincerity is a GREAT way to be a lousy friend. When your friends can't take your word on something or when they can't believe what you say, then they won't be your friends for long.

Jesus says, "Do not swear by your head, for you cannot make even one hair white or black. All you need to say is simply 'Yes,' or 'No'; anything beyond this comes from the evil one" (Matthew 5:36-37, TNIV). Jesus isn't talking about the kind of swearing like saying curse words. He's talking about saying, "I swear it's true!"

Jesus is saying that if you just speak honestly all the time, then you'll never need to say, "I swear." If your "yes" is always honest, and if your "no" is always honest, your friends will never have a reason to ask, "Do you promise you're telling the truth?"

So if you want to be a stupid, smelly, hurtful, and horrible friend, then be insincere. Really—we mean it. We swear we're telling the truth. No—really. You can trust us!

SMOTHERING

Every year after Thanksgiving, I (Marko) live in food-happiness-land for about a week—or until the gravy runs out. I don't make a traditional plate of Thanksgiving leftovers: I have a weird little personal favorite. I put some turkey into a bowl or on a piece of bread. Then I put stuffing or mashed potatoes (depending on which we have more of) all over it. Then, I *smother* the whole mess in gravy, nuke it in the microwave, and put myself into a flavor coma.

My family laughs at me for another meal I make for myself once in a while—the Marko's Specialty Hot, Open-Face, Smothered Sandwich. Here's the recipe:

- One slice of bread, placed in the middle of a large plate

- A dab o' ranch dressing or barbecue sauce (optional)

- A double portion of meat. Turkey and roast beef are my favorites.

- And here's the kicker: mounds of shredded cheese. Sliced cheese works also, but shredded cheese is easier. (Weird fact: When Kurt and I were kids, you couldn't buy shredded cheese in the store—you had to shred it yourself!)

- Microwave it and then sit down to a hot and gooey, *smothered* mess of wonderfulness.

See, smothering can be a good thing when it comes to food. (You might not agree with Marko's particular *smothered* recipes, but you could probably come up with your own.) But smothering isn't so helpful when it comes to friendship.

To *smother* another person is...well...just think of it as being the gravy or the melted cheese. Smothering another person is not giving them any space, demanding all their attention and time, and feeling threatened if they have any other friends besides you.

Friendships, just like people, need to breathe. Friendships need space. Friends who are together 24/7/365 are likely *not* in a healthy friendship. And most people don't really want that kind of friendship anyhow. So, if you demand that kind of time and attention from your friends, you'll probably end up scaring them away. Seriously, being a smothering friend is one of the most common reasons why middle school friendships end.

So if you want lousy friendships that don't last very long, or if you want to be a *bad friend*, then be the melty cheese. Or the gravy. It's your choice.

"SOMETIMES I TRY TOO HARD TO MAKE FRIENDS, AND IT ENDS UP FREAKING THEM OUT."

—NOAH, 6TH GRADE

I WAS A MIDDLE SCHOOL DORK!
—MARKO

A bunch of my friends and I were at a retreat—I think it was with our middle school youth group from church. My friends and I loved playing pranks. Mostly, we loved playing pranks on other people. But when we ran out of those ideas, we'd play pranks on each other.

I'm sure if I really strained my brain, I could remember the slow build-up to battle that led to this stupidest-of-all-stupids story. Like, my friend John probably put pine needles in my sleeping bag or something like that. Something that was just begging for all-out, full-scale, warlike retaliation. At least I'm sure that's what I was thinking.

John—somehow my best friend through all those years and still a close friend of mine to this day—was a small guy. So many of my brilliant prank ideas on John had something to do with lifting him. Because I could.

It was after "lights out," and all the guys were in their sleeping bags. It's been many years, and my memory is missing a few little bits here—like, I have no idea where our cabin counselor was, or why he didn't stop the idiocy. But, whatever.

I snuck over to John's bunk, shoved him down into his sleeping bag, and twisted the top together like the top of a bread bag. He kicked and screamed and stuff—but he really couldn't do anything. Besides, he was always up for some kind of adventure.

I recruited a few friends, and we carried John—still balled up in his sleeping bag—outside. We carried him to the center of camp where there was a tall flagpole (can you see it coming?). Yup, we then tied the end of the flag rope around the top of John's sleeping bag and made sure the knot was really secure (safety first!). Then the four of us pulled and pulled, and we hauled John—still in his sleeping bag—all the way up the flag-pole. Oh, and he wasn't quite sure what was happening. He later told me he could tell our voices were getting further away, but he didn't know why.

Here's where the story goes, well, downhill. We thought we were hilarious. We thought we were the funniest guys on the planet. Until the rope slipped a tiny bit in our hands. Then we just panicked. We couldn't hold the rope anymore! Our hands were cramping up, and the rope was thin and getting slippery in our now-sweaty hands. So we—ready?—we let go. Yup. We just let go of the rope, and John—still in his sleeping bag—came falling back toward earth. And he landed right on that little square of concrete just below the flagpole.

John broke his arm, but that was all. And we were all pretty lucky—especially John! It's now been 30 years since this happened, and I was just visiting with John recently. We were talking about this story, and once again John said, "I can't believe you let go of the rope!" Yeah, well, I was a middle school dork, remember?

TOUGH SITUATIONS

WHEN YOUR PARENTS DON'T LIKE YOUR FRIENDS

Have you ever had anything like this happen?

You finish a phone call with a new friend of yours, and your mom asks, "Who were you talking to?" You tell her it was Kyle, and she responds, "Oh, I don't like that Kyle."

Or you ask your dad if he'll give you a ride to the mall. Your dad asks who you're going with, and you tell him Tasha. He says, "No, I don't want you hanging out at the mall with Tasha. She's a bad influence on you."

It's hard when your parents don't like your friends. It leaves you in a really tough spot of trying to defend your friend to your parents, or choosing between your parents and your friend. And that's always hard, whether or not your parents are right about your friend.

It seems to us there are two basic groupings here: Really good friends whom your parents don't like, and not-very-good friends whom your parents also don't like. Let's start with the second group because it's a little bit easier. (It's never simple, though.)

Here's the deal: As hard as it might be to believe, your parents are *probably* right more often than they're wrong. Sure, this isn't true for all parents; but *most* parents have their kids' best interests in mind and a decent sense of who's a good friend for their children and who isn't. No doubt your parents have had experiences with people who *seemed* like good friends at the time, but then these friends actually led your parents to make choices and do stuff that wasn't good for them.

So our somewhat stupid answer for a situation like this (because you probably won't do it) is to listen to your parents. Of course, that's easy for us to say—we're just writing a book, not living your life.

In the other situation (where your parents don't like a friend of yours, but the friend *really is* a good friend and *not* a bad influence on you), there are a few things you can try, like:

- Ask if you can invite the friend over to have dinner with your family. If your parents get to know your friend better, they might start to view your relationship differently.

- Try to have a productive conversation with your parents—one that's *not* loaded with emotions and yelling or whining—about why you want this person as a friend. Listen as your parents explain their concerns, and then take those concerns seriously.

- Pray! Ask God to either change your parents' minds or help you see that your parents are right. Be open to whichever answer God provides.

WHEN YOUR FRIENDS ARE FIGHTING *(STUCK IN THE MIDDLE)*

You can't feel much worse than the way you feel when you're stuck in the middle of two friends who are fighting. And if it hasn't happened to you yet, it will. Unfortunately, when it happens, you usually end up being the one everybody's mad at. Conflict among friends is unavoidable, and being stuck between two fighting friends is just as hard to avoid.

We'll make you a promise: You WILL find yourself in the middle of an argument between two of your friends. But you don't have to *stay* stuck in the middle. It's possible to get yourself out of this really tough situation. Here are a couple of ideas:

Try not to take sides. When they're arguing, your friends may purposely try to draw you and other mutual friends onto their side. A classic technique for winning an argument is to be able to say, "See, all these people agree with me!" In certain situations (usually with the bigger, more serious disagreements) it may become necessary for you to take sides and share your thoughts, but most of the time you're better off trying to stay out of the argument altogether.

Encourage your friends to talk to each other directly. One of the reasons you'll find yourself stuck in the middle is because your friends will often talk to each other through you. One friend will tell you to tell him so he can tell her. It's surprisingly easy to become the messenger for stuff your friends really need to talk about face to face. The

Bible tells us we're always supposed to talk to people we disagree with face to face and not pull others into our disagreements unless we really have to (Matthew 18:15-17).

Ask somebody older and wiser to step in. When you feel like you're stuck in the middle, it may be wise to ask someone like a parent, teacher, youth leader, or youth pastor to step in and help iron things out. The good thing about doing this is you can help your friends without being forced to take sides in the disagreement.

Your friends will fight. You'll find yourself in the middle. But you don't have to remain stuck there.

WHEN YOUR FRIENDS START MAKING BAD CHOICES

This is a tough one. (And we suppose it should be, since we included it in the section called "Tough Situations." Duh! Aren't we brilliant?)

Recently, a guy in Marko's small group tearfully shared how his friend was expelled from school because he got caught with pot. And the guy in Marko's group didn't even know his friend had ever tried pot.

When a friend starts making bad choices, here's the first question you have to ask yourself: *Am I strong enough to stay friends with this person and not start making the same bad choices?* This is a *huge* question. You can love the friend and try to help her; but first you have to know whether or not you might be tempted to try the same thing—whatever it is. (Remember, the influence of our friends can be really, really powerful! Read more about this in chapters 8 and 42, if you haven't already.)

If you *do* think you might be tempted—either to try something you shouldn't or to make the same bad decisions as your friend—then you *have to* make the tough choice and put some distance in that friendship. It may be the only way you can protect yourself from making bad choices.

I (Marko) remember a time in high school when a friend of mine was really getting into drinking alcohol. He was a friend who had a lot of influence on me because I always thought he was so cool, and I kinda wanted to be like him. But I could tell that if I kept hanging out with this friend, I'd probably start drinking with him. So I sat down with him and had a really hard conversation about needing to take a break from spending time together because I didn't think I was strong enough to not go along with the choices he was making. (I still remember his response, by the way. He said, "That's cool. I just have a few good party years left, and then I'll get serious about Jesus.")

If you *do* choose to put a little distance into a friendship, that doesn't mean you have to totally cut yourself off from that friend. You can still talk to her and even hang out—just not in a situation where you think she might make that bad choice, whatever it is. Having the guts to say something like this could really make a difference in your friend's life.

And even if you *do* think you're strong enough *not* to allow your friend to lead you into making the same bad choice, it's important for you to talk to your friend and let her know how you feel. Really, you're being a lousy friend if you don't speak up in a situation like this. You know that saying, "Friends don't let friends drive drunk?" It's the same idea: If you're really a friend, then you'll speak up about your friend's harmful choice.

"FRIENDS ARE IMPORTANT, BUT IF THEY'RE TRYING TO GET YOU TO DO STUFF YOU SHOULDN'T, IT'S PROBABLY TIME TO FIND SOME NEW ONES."
—ROBBIE, 8TH GRADE

WHEN YOUR FRIENDS GET HURT *(SOMETHING BAD HAPPENS)*

When something bad happens to your friend, it's time for you to really step up on what it means to be a friend. Here's the kind of stuff we're talking about:

- Your friend's parents get a divorce or they're fighting all the time.

- Your friend gets abused in some way: physically, sexually, verbally, or emotionally.

- Someone your friend cares about dies, or gets a serious disease, or gets in a serious accident.

- Your friend loses something really important to her—maybe her house burns down or things are stolen from her.

- Your friend's sibling gets in trouble with the law or has some other kind of major problem.

- Your friend starts making super-destructive choices, like cutting, starving herself (anorexia or bulimia), or thinking about suicide.

The first thing you have to ask yourself—just like we youth workers do—is this: *Is my friend in danger of getting hurt again or could she hurt someone else?* If the answer is yes (like, if your friend is thinking of suicide, or if your friend is being abused), then you HAVE TO tell a responsible adult. This is really hard to do because you might feel like you're not keeping her secret. But if you really care about your friend, you simply have to do this.

You could start with a trustworthy youth worker from your church, or you could go to a school guidance counselor (they know what to do in situations like this). It's great if you can do this *with* your friend. Remember: If something serious happened to your friend and you *didn't* try to stop it, then you'd struggle with that guilt for the rest of your life.

Next, it's important to talk about the situation with your friend. Ask her to share what's going on and how she feels. Oftentimes, people who are hurting don't know if it's okay to talk about the hurt in their lives. And talking about hurt can be so very helpful.

Encourage your friend to find an adult she can talk to (no matter how serious or not serious the problem seems)—and volunteer to go with her. You shouldn't be expected to understand or know exactly how to deal with difficult situations like these. You can't be your friend's therapist or doctor—not even her problem solver. But you can be a friend who helps her take a step in the right direction.

Whatever you do, don't ignore the problem. Good friends don't do that, even if it seems like the easier thing to do.

WHEN YOU DON'T HAVE ANY FRIENDS

If this is the tough situation you find yourself in, we want you to know—REALLY KNOW—that you're not alone. We don't mean you should just stop feeling lonely and stuff. We *do mean* that we've been where you are—both Marko and Kurt—and there are lots of other people your own age who've also experienced this.

We also mean this: Jesus is a friend to those who don't have friends. Yes, Jesus wants to be a friend to everyone. But if you read the story of Jesus' life in the Bible (a great thing to do if you're feeling friendless), you'll see that he seems to have a special soft spot in his heart for people without friends.

Check out the story of Jesus and Zacchaeus (Luke 19:1-10). Zack was a tax collector, which means everyone else hated him—*everyone*. Well, everyone except Jesus. When Jesus passed by the spot where Zack was hiding in a tree (just to catch a glimpse of Jesus), Jesus stopped and talked to Zack. (There were tons of people there, and they watched and listened to see what Jesus was going to say to Zack. This must have been a pretty awkward moment for everyone *except* Jesus.) And then—this is the amazing part—Jesus invited himself over to Zack's house for lunch. No one had ever done that with Zack before, and it changed Zack's life!

Read the parts of this book about how to be a good friend and how to make friends (sections 7 and 10, for starters). Then try to be on the lookout for people who might make good friends. Don't just look to the popular crowd or the cool kids. Look for other kids who don't have friends. And especially look for someone you might have something in common with—maybe you think you'd be into the same things. That's often the beginning point of friendships—sharing a common interest.

Making friends requires some courage because it's risky. The person you try to make friends with might blow you off or hurt your feelings. We admit this is difficult—but it's the only way toward starting new friendships.

Most importantly, don't give up! We were designed for friendships. We weren't made to be alone.

WHEN YOUR FRIENDS TURN AGAINST YOU

Have you ever seen the TV show *When Animals Attack?* A person will be playing in his front yard with his fun, energetic, happy pit bull (yes, pit bulls can be fun), and then suddenly the dog will attack him for no clear reason and try to bite his face off. It's crazy!

Our friends can be a lot like pit bulls. You can be having a fun, happy, problem-free relationship and then BAAAM! Your friend turns against you and tries to bite your face off! You're left to stagger away wondering, *What did I do to deserve this? What went wrong?*

We understand this can be a super-painful experience. So let's take a look at some things that might help the next time a friend turns against you.

Look around. Analyze the situation. Are you in different stages of life now? Has your friend or you experienced any drastic changes? Is your friend trying to fit in with a different crowd? Does your friend or you have a new "special somebody"? Did you do something to your friend? Lots of stuff can put a strain on your friendship and cause your friend to turn against you. Then again, there's always the possibility that there's no good reason for the sudden change in your friend's behavior.

Talk to your friend. Losing a friend can be a very tough thing, especially if it's a very close friend. So take the first step in talking about the issue and keeping the friendship. Don't try to pay her back by giving her the silent treatment. Ask questions: *What went wrong? Did I do something?* If it was something you did, apologize and ask for forgiveness. If she doesn't want to talk, leave a message on her cell phone or send her an e-mail. She might just need some time before she's willing to talk about it.

Be prepared. It hurts when a friend turns against you, and it might signal the end of the relationship. Even though losing a friend hurts, it isn't the end of the world. (It just feels like it is.) You'll find new friends—no doubt about it. Learn to rely on the ultimate Friend, Jesus Christ. Read his Word (the Bible), talk to him about it, and ask him to help you. He'll always give you the strength to make it through the loss of a friend.

Friends can be like fish (minus the fins and scales). You may have heard the old saying, "There are other fish in the sea." Well, it's true! You're going to lose a fish every now and then—it might flop off the hook or snap the line. But if you're patient, eventually you'll catch another fish—or two or three. Fish can only resist the bait for so long. Who knows, you might even catch the same fish again!

Okay, enough of the dumb "friends are like fish" example. You get the point.

WHEN YOU *HAVE* TO END A FRIENDSHIP

Take some time to think about your friends and ask yourself this: *Are there any friends I* shouldn't *hang out with?* If you only have one friend to think about, this will be easy. If you have tons of friends, this could take a few minutes.

There are times when you just know you *have* to end a friendship. Sometimes the reasons are as clear as day; other times you're not sure about the reason, you just *feel it.* Let's take a look at some of the "clear-as-day" reasons to end a friendship.

Building up versus tearing down. There's nothing positive about hanging around negative people—they'll only tear you down. You need friends who will see the positives in tough situations and help you see them as well. Some other "tear down" qualities to watch out for in your friends are disrespect, not accepting you for who you are, stabbing you in the back, and involvement in drugs or alcohol. If any of these qualities are common with a friend (even after you've talked to him about it), you probably need to end the friendship. Remember, if a friend isn't building you up, then he's probably tearing you down.

God's way versus the world's way. Take a moment and picture a two-lane highway. Traffic in one lane travels in one direction, while traffic in the other lane travels in the opposite direction. Life is a lot like a two-lane highway—there are only two ways you can go, and they go in opposite directions. One direction is God's way, which is everything that is pure, right, and pleasing to God. The other direction is, well, everything that goes against God's principles and his purpose for your life. You can't go in both directions at the same time. If a friend (especially a close friend) is leading you away from God, then you probably need to end the friendship.

Your friends influence you, so you need to end a friendship if a friend is pointing you in the wrong direction. When you do, make sure you're honest about why you're ending the relationship, and then end it in a way that shows you still care about your friend.

WHEN YOU *WANT* TO END A FRIENDSHIP

It's our opinion that people walk away from friendships too easily and, oftentimes, for the wrong reasons. Wanting to end a friendship for the right reasons is an okay—even a natural—thing. But if you want to end a friendship just because she wore the same outfit you did without asking for your permission first, then you may need to rethink your decision.

Here are a few things to think about before you decide to end a friendship:

Hang in there. Give it time. Friendships can go through a funk, and it just takes some time to get out of it. Be patient with your friend. Use this experience to learn more about yourself and your friend. Make sure you look at yourself—are you being selfish or unfair in the friendship? Sometimes the roots of a struggle stem from our own behaviors or choices, but we don't realize it, so we put the blame on our friends instead.

Learn to forgive. Even as your friendships grow deeper, there will be times when you want to end a friendship because your friend has wronged you. Learn to forgive your friend instead. First, because it's what God wants you to do. And second, because you're going to need your friend's forgiveness at some point. Practice the art of giving your friend second, third, and forty-third chances.

Think and talk it through. When you want to end a friendship, make sure you've given it some thought. Think about the reasons why you want to end it and write them down. After you've thought it through for a while, talk to your friend about it. Talking about some of the reasons why you want to end the friendship gives your friend a chance to respond and explain some of the stuff that's bothering you.

Friendships can be wacky. Your friendships will change. You'll lose friends, and you'll get new friends. It's all part of life. And it's okay to choose to end a friendship.

When middle school friendships end, things usually get ugly and feelings get hurt. That's not as likely to happen if you've shown patience, hung in there, been forgiving, and talked things through.

WHAT TO DO IF YOU'RE SHY

Are you outgoing? Do you enjoy being around a lot of people? Do you like to talk to people you don't even know? Do you love getting called on by the teacher in class? Do you try out for every school play? Do you usually talk really loud? If you answered "no" to all of these questions, you're probably a shy person.

There's nothing wrong with being shy. It's actually pretty common among middle schoolers. But when it comes to friendships, shyness (along with a lot of other things) can become a barrier. The good news is it doesn't have to be an obstacle for you.

Let's take a look at how being shy can be an okay thing in existing friendships, as well as when you're finding new ones.

Thrive within your comfort zone. Be yourself and utilize your strengths. Discover what you're gifted at doing and use those gifts. If you don't really like to talk but love to write, communicate with your friends by writing tons of notes, letters, and e-mails. You can even make new friends by writing letters. If you play soccer, use that gift to meet others on your soccer team. Most shy people make really good friends because they don't need to talk all the time. If you're shy, you're probably a pretty good listener, which is one of the best qualities a friend can have.

Try stepping out of your comfort zone. You probably knew we were going to say this. In fact, you've probably heard it many times before. This is a tough thing to do even if you're not shy because it makes us uncomfortable when we do it. But look for opportunities to stretch yourself. Give your testimony at church so people can get to know you better. Go on a mission trip or to a camp with a group of students from your church. It's difficult to live with people for a whole week and not develop some sort of friendship. Take small steps and slowly look for ways you can come out of your shell. Stepping out of your comfort zone can really build up your self-confidence. Give it a shot!

If you're shy, don't panic. Part of your shyness is the way God wired you. God also wired you to have friends, so don't let your shyness get in the way.

HOW TO
MAKE FRIENDS

MEETING PEOPLE FOR THE FIRST TIME

What do I say? How do I act? This is really awkward! Is he going to like me? Will she think I'm stupid? Will I fit in? These are the kinds of things most middle schoolers ask themselves when they're meeting people for the first time. Other middle schoolers never ask themselves those questions—they just jump right in. Love it or hate it, meeting new people is part of being a person yourself. Here are a few ideas to help make it a little less freaky.

Introduce yourself. As simple as this idea sounds, in the nervousness of the moment, people often forget to give their names. Start off by simply introducing yourself: *Hey, my name is* (insert your name here). This shows the person that you want her to know who you are, and that you hope to get to know her.

Ask a question. If it looks like the person is interested in getting to know you, ask him a question or two. Don't bombard him with 1,000 questions, but toss out a couple to help spark the conversation. Questions like, *What class do you have next? How long have you lived here? What are your hobbies? Do you believe in extraterrestrial life forms, and, if so, how likely is it that they're making plans to invade Earth—RIGHT NOW?* (Okay, that last one probably isn't a good icebreaker question.) Asking a few simple questions is a great way to get the ball rolling. If he ignores your questions, rolls his eyes at you, or points at you and starts laughing hysterically, then you can pretty much assume he isn't real interested in being friends. That's okay. At least you met somebody new.

Be yourself. When you meet someone for the first time, don't try to be someone you're not. You want her to know who you *really* are, after all, and you can't go on pretending to be someone you're not forever. If you begin to spend a lot of time with her, she'll eventually discover you're a different person, and the friendship probably won't last. Acting like somebody you aren't— even if you're just trying to make a new friend—is a surefire way to mess up a friendship down the road. Be yourself. It's better for the real you to be rejected than for the fake you to be accepted.

You're going to meet hundreds and hundreds of people in your lifetime. Some of the people you meet will become your friends, but most of them won't. Either way, practicing the stuff you've just read will help along the way.

MAKING YOURSELF FRIENDSHIP-WORTHY

A good friendship starts with one person: You! While it's important to ask yourself what kinds of friends you want to have (we'll talk about that a little later), it may be more important to ask yourself what kind of friend you want to *be*.

One of the secrets of healthy, long-lasting friendships is for you to be a really good friend yourself. Earlier in this book we listed a whole bunch of ways you can be a good friend; we even wrote an entire chapter about each one. Take another look at the list:

- Loyalty or faithfulness

- Honesty

- Encouragement

- Giving and serving

- Compassion

- Listening

- Attentiveness

- Fun!

- Flexibility

- Accountability

Way too often, people make the mistake of expecting their friends to have these qualities without realizing *they* need to have them, too. You want your friends to be loyal? Then start by being a loyal friend to them. You want your friends to be encouraging? Then lead the way by cheering them on.

Even though a good friendship starts with *you*, you really can't do it alone. You need God's help. One or two of these qualities may come pretty easily for you, but you can probably pick several from the list that don't. God wants to help you grow in these difficult areas so you can get better at being a good friend. It's not easy. In fact it's way easier to have an attitude that says, *Hey, you're pretty lucky I'm even considering being friends with you. So you'd better work hard to make this relationship happen.*

The Bible says that if you want to have friends, then you have to be friendly (Proverbs 18:24). In other words, the best way to have good friendships is to start by being a good friend yourself.

"MY MOM TELLS ME THE BEST WAY TO HAVE GOOD FRIENDS IS TO BE A GOOD FRIEND. I DON'T TOTALLY GET THAT, BUT IT KINDA MAKES SENSE."

—JOEY, 6TH GRADE

COMMON INTERESTS

We (Marko and Kurt) became friends because we had a common interest (something we both liked): We both enjoyed working with middle school students. Really, that's how we got to know each other. We started with something we had in common, and we built a friendship around it.

That's really one of the easiest—and most normal—ways of making new friends. But it's usually a new idea to middle schoolers. (Check out chapter 2, "Shifting Friendships," to learn why.)

Of course, that means you have to start by thinking about what interests you. It might be really obvious to you, or it might not be. Because you're changing so much right now, it's easy to feel a bit "in between" about what you like. For example, you know you *used* to be into dolls or into tiny metal toy cars, but you aren't *really* into those things anymore (at least you may not want to admit to anyone that you are).

So are you into a sport? Or maybe you're into a certain kind of video game? Or music? If your interests are too narrow, you might want to think a bit more broadly. Like, if your passion—the thing you're more into than anything else—is Russian matryoshka dolls from the late 1800s...well, you're *probably* not going to make a bunch of new friends if you stand on a table in the middle of your cafeteria and yell, "Attention, everyone! Can I have your attention, please? I really, *really* love Russian matryoshka dolls. You know, those stacking dolls?

Little wooden dolls shaped like eggs that you can open up and find an even smaller doll inside? But I only like the ones from the late 1800s. I think about them all the time. I even dream about them. And if there's anyone else here who is *also* into Russian stacking dolls from the 1800s, I'd be very interested in considering a friendship with you. I have applications right over here."

Yeah. You get the idea. The only friend you might get by doing this is the kid who thinks, *I love doing really stupid things like making announcements while standing on a lunchroom table, too!*

You get the point: Look for people who like the same things you do. This isn't rocket science. (Well, not unless you're interested in rocket science, of course!)

> "SOMETIMES GOOD FRIENDSHIPS ARE HARD WORK, BUT I COULDN'T IMAGINE LIFE WITHOUT THEM."
> —CASSIE, 8TH GRADE

ASKING QUESTIONS

We can't think of a more important skill in the art of making friends than asking questions. We know it sounds kind of silly and simple—but it really is a *huge* factor. And asking questions isn't something that comes naturally to most young teenagers. But the good news is it's something you can totally learn.

Even a total jerk can make friends if he's willing to ask a few questions.

Here's why—when you ask someone a question, you do a few things:

- You show you're interested in her, not just yourself.

- You give her permission to talk about herself—something most of us love to do!

- And you create a little space for a conversation that might not happen otherwise. In other words, you make it possible to spend a minute or two together (while the question is being answered).

That's a lot of stuff! Wow! Seriously, maybe now you can see why asking questions is so powerful when you're making friends.

So, how 'bout some tips on asking good questions...

First, remember that simple questions are often the best. If you don't know someone but you walk up to her and ask, "Please, would you be willing to talk for a few minutes about whether you prefer independent films or mass-produced Hollywood films?" then you'll probably get a look that says, "Freak!" and not much more. A simple, more natural question is often a follow-up question. Like, if someone says something, you can say, "Really? What do you mean?"

Second, ask questions about the person (but don't get too personal if you don't know her). Asking someone you don't know what kind of deodorant she uses? Bad idea. Asking someone you don't know what kind of music he's into? Good idea. Get the idea?

Finally, don't become the annoying question-asking kid. In other words, while asking questions is probably the most important thing you can do to make new friends, you can also overdo it. If you're constantly asking questions when someone clearly isn't interested in talking to you, you'll just become an annoyance. Like a pesky little dog or something. Yip, yip, yip! Don't be the yippy little dog.

BEING AWARE OF POTENTIAL FRIENDS

Can you imagine walking around your school all day with your eyes closed or while wearing a blindfold and trying to find people to start a friendship with? Wow—that would be almost impossible, wouldn't it? You bump into someone and ask, "Will you be my friend?" Oops, that was the lunch lady, the one with only one tooth. She answers, "Okay, I'll be your friend." You open one eye a little bit, realize what you've done, and run away, vowing to never show your face in the cafeteria again.

Of course—let's state the obvious—you have to keep your eyes open if you want to see potential new friends. But "having your eyes open" is more than just propping open your droopy little eyelids. If you want to start new friendships, you have to install some fresh batteries in your potential-friend-awareness sensor. No, they don't really make those. (Duh!) But we think you get the idea: You have to be aware of who might be a good potential friend for you.

Being aware of potential friends means using a couple of your senses:

Look. See who's interested in the same things you are. See who hangs out in the places where you hang out. See who might not have lots of friends already.

Listen. Hear what a potential friend says or doesn't say. Listen to what she talks about. Ask her questions, and listen to the answers to see if she's the kind of person who would make a good friend for you.

That's probably it—unless you want to use your sense of smell to see if they stink or smell good. Let's not even mention taste, okay?

> "YOU CAN HAVE MORE THAN ONE BEST FRIEND."
>
> —A. J., 7TH GRADE

PICKING THE RIGHT POTENTIAL FRIENDS

Ooh, this is a tough one. It's hard for us to write, and we think it'll be a little hard to understand. So let's all watch TV instead. No, we're just kidding! Kinda.

Here's the blunt, honest, difficult, challenging, not-easy-to-say-and-even-harder-to-hear reality: Many young teenagers absolutely stink at figuring out who would make a good friend. Sorry. We really didn't like writing that. But after working with tens of thousands of teenagers, we can't even tell you how many hundreds or thousands of times we've seen teenagers make super-lousy choices about someone they pursue as a potential new friend.

The biggest mistake we've seen students make in this area is assuming the popular kids in school (or wherever) would make the best new friends. We know there are lots of reasons for this. Many times teenagers try to become friends with popular kids because they think it'll make *them* popular, too. Just remember, the most popular kids—

- Often don't have the slightest desire for any more friends. They have all the friends they could ever need.

- Are often some of the meanest people around. Of course, that's not always true. But we've seen it over and over again—if you try to make friends with a super-popular kid, you'll probably end up getting hurt.

So, when you're *looking* and *listening* (read the previous chapter, if you haven't already) for potential new friends, *look* and *listen* for potential friends who would be a good friendship fit for you. You know who you are, right? You know what you like and don't like. You know what things interest you and what doesn't. You know what your values are—what's important to you.

Remember—we've said this over and over—friends who have stuff in common have a better chance of building a good, long-lasting friendship. That doesn't mean you can't have some differences and still have a great friendship. But you *have* to have *some* stuff in common.

One more thought here: All of us become a little bit like our friends (or a lot like our friends). So be *really* careful when considering your possible new friends, and pick people you wouldn't mind becoming like. Don't start a friendship with someone who'll lead you to become a person you don't want to be.

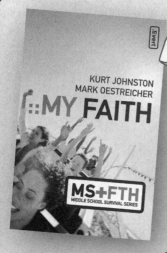

KURT JOHNSTON
MARK OESTREICHER

::MY FAITH

MS+FTH
MIDDLE SCHOOL SURVIVAL SERIES

LIFE AND FAITH CAN BE HARD WHEN YOU'RE IN MIDDLE SCHOOL. BUT THIS BOOK GIVES YOU ALL THE TIPS AND SECRETS YOU NEED TO REALLY GRASP YOUR FAITH AND KEEP HOLD OF IT.

My Faith
Middle School Survival Series
Kurt Johnston & Mark Oestreicher

RETAIL $9.99
ISBN 0-310-27382-X

EVERYTHING IS CHANGING—INCLUDING THE WAY YOUR FAMILY INTERACTS. THIS BOOK WILL GIVE YOU SECRETS AND TIPS TO HELP MAKE YOUR FAMILY EVEN BETTER AND SURVIVE THE CHANGES THAT COME ALONG WITH MIDDLE SCHOOL.

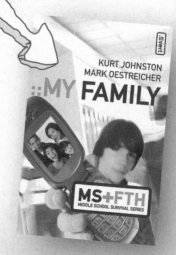

KURT JOHNSTON
MARK OESTREICHER

::MY FAMILY

MS+FTH
MIDDLE SCHOOL SURVIVAL SERIES

My Family
Middle School Survival Series
Kurt Johnston & Mark Oestreicher

RETAIL $9.99
ISBN 0-310-27430-3

Visit www.invertbooks.com or your local bookstore.

LISTEN TO WHAT JESUS HAS TO SAY TO YOU. IN THIS 60-DAY DEVO YOU'LL RECEIVE DAILY LETTERS FROM JESUS AND SPEND SOME TIME JOURNALING YOUR THOUGHTS BACK TO HIM AS YOU TAKE PART IN THE CONVERSATION.

Conversations with Jesus
Getting in on God's Story
Youth for Christ

RETAIL $10.99
ISBN 0-310-27346-3

.invert

Visit www.invertbooks.com or your local bookstore.

MOST TEENAGERS THINK THAT BEING A CHRISTIAN MEANS DOING THE RIGHT THING. BUT FIGURING OUT WHAT THE "RIGHT THING" IS CAN BE A CHALLENGE. IT'S DIFFICULT FOR STUDENTS TO TELL THE DIFFERENCE BETWEEN GOD'S PLAN FOR THEM AND WHAT OTHER CHRISTIANS SAY IS GOD'S PLAN FOR THEM. AUTHOR MARK MATLOCK WILL GUIDE YOUR STUDENTS THROUGH GOD'S WORD TO HELP THEM FIGURE OUT WHAT GOD REALLY WANTS FROM THEM.

What Does God Want from Me?
Understanding God's Desire for Your Life
Mark Matlock
RETAIL $9.99
ISBN 0-310-25815-4

invert